EXTREME TEAMMATES

Darren Barndt

ISBN: 978-1-699228-99-9

ACKNOWLEDGEMENTS

To my wife, Brenda, thank you for being exactly who you are. To my sons, Marcus, Michael, and Steven, each of you with your own extreme talents, I hope you always share those talents with each other, with other people, and with the world. I challenge you to always believe in yourself, to believe in the power of people working together, and to make your own impact on humanity. To my parents, looking down from above, thank you.

CONTENTS

Darren Barndt

Introduction

It's hard to imagine my life without sports. They have had a significant impact on me throughout my childhood, my youth, and my professional career. They still do. I have benefited greatly from what a simple game has to offer. As I grew older, I became fascinated with the impact of sports on people, on teams, and on society. Nelson Mandela summed it up perfectly when he said, "Sport has the power to change the world. It has the power to inspire, the power to unite people in a way that little else does. It speaks to youth in a language they understand. Sport can create hope, where there was once only despair. It is more powerful than governments in breaking down racial barriers."

I grew up in southern Illinois playing baseball and basketball. I loved football, but my school was too small for a team. My childhood was filled with great friends and great friendships, but sports were a defining feature, both my chief leisure activity and my primary motivator. They provided thrills, structure, discipline, and joy.

For most of my childhood, sports were my life. I played on winning teams and losing teams. I suffered through seasons where we lost almost every game, and in other seasons I played in championship contests. Even as a child I wondered, why was one team successful and others were not? Was it the players or the coaching? Was it always about physical talent or did mental capacity have a role in the process? I didn't know it at the time, but I would obsess over this question for decades.

I played baseball for two years at Lincoln Trail College and then transferred to Southern Illinois University at Carbondale. I was twenty years old and knew that I would need to change my focus as an athlete. I shifted my dreams to coaching. My love of sports wouldn't stop with my own abilities. I dreamed of coaching basketball and pursued that dream. For two years I worked for the Southern Illinois basketball program. In this role, I was fortunate to be part of a great program. I sat on the bench when we played Duke in the first round of the NCAA tournament way back in 1993.

I graduated and got into public education, still keeping my eye on coaching. I moved to Olney, Illinois, where I coached football and basketball. Then I headed to Kansas, Illinois, where I became the varsity basketball and baseball coach. I worked hard as a teacher and even harder as a coach. I loved it.

In 2000, I moved to Chicago and got a job at Lake Forest High School. I was still teaching and coaching multiple sports, but my passion was always basketball because it involves only a handful of players, individuals that can work together to shape and impact a game.

I used to believe that only certain people had potential for leadership, and that only with the perfect hand-picked leaders would a team have a chance at lasting success. I was completely and utterly wrong on both counts, and I wrote this book in part because I realized most people believe these exact same falsehoods.

I kept up with my professional practice, and I eventually earned a Master's degree in educational leadership and became an administrator. I also kept coaching.

Being an administrator is, in many ways, similar to being a coach. I have a lot of responsibilities in both roles, but the primary work—the teaching in the classroom, the playing of the game—is done by others. My job has evolved. I am now more of a facilitator. Just as I no longer rebound or take grounders, I also no longer grade papers. Coaching is not playing. Administrating is not teaching. But in both leadership capacities I get to develop new talent, pass on what I've learned, and help shape the future.

As an administrator, one of my primary responsibilities is to evaluate teachers. We use a highly regarded evaluation model called the Danielson Framework, a powerful tool. Danielson encourages, measures, and supports the growth of both students and educators. In the Danielson Framework, a teacher's rating is determined, in part, by how well students work as a team—by how well they teach each other, encourage others, and enforce the classroom's standards. The best teachers create an environment where students are driving their own learning.

Over the years, I've read dozens and dozens of books about coaching, sports psychology, and education. I've coached hundreds, if not thousands, of games and thousands of players in different sports and different places. I've studied, observed, learned. I've seen a lot in my coaching years—new trends, new diets, new approaches to exercise, new strategies, rediscoveries of old tactics.

After about twenty-five years of coaching, tons of research, and plenty of reflection, I finally realized that everyone has the capacity to do two things: be a great teammate and be a great leader. And I realized that the two things are connected.

I believe that if you can measure your expectations, you can more easily manage them, so I set out to design a system that makes better teammates, that helps people define, improve, and assess their ability to achieve greatness as a collective group. Notice I didn't say do just a little bit better, or clock in slightly higher on a bar graph. I said greatness, and that is what we are after: a system that can turn your team into something remarkable.

My career as a coach has informed my career as an administrator and vice versa, a fortunate synergy that led me to discover that the Danielson Framework could be applied, but also amplified, to create a new system for teamwork, a system I call Extreme Teammates. This system works for every kind of team—sports, business, family, etc.

This book is my way of sharing what I've learned, my way of trying to make the world a bit better. Because I believe in sports. I believe sports bring people together. I believe sports make people stronger and more resilient. I believe sports give people confidence and discipline and rigor and also joy, even euphoria. I think back on my own days as a young player, hitting rocks with a broomstick or playing 3-on-3 with my friends, and I know how formative sports can be to a young psyche. If we pay attention, sports can show all of us, from the benchwarmer to the star athlete, how to be a better teammate, a better leader, a better person.

This book will provide a structure and system of strategies to transform your team or organization into a team of leaders instead of a team of followers. These tools will motivate, inspire, and teach every person how to become a great teammate. The Seven Key Strategies of Extreme Teammates will challenge you to move from ordinary to extraordinary, from comfortable to uncomfortable, from selfish to selfless, from quiet to vocal, and from stagnant to intentional. I will demonstrate how to use our framework to identify strengths and weaknesses, measure your growth and inspire others towards greatness. Master these strategies—and it's easier than it sounds, as each strategy leads into the next—and you will be an extreme teammate. Apply these to your team, spread them to your teammates, and you will achieve great things.

Ideal for sports teams as well as businesses, the Extreme Teammate Pyramid, located in the Appendix, has twenty-one clearly defined expectations or qualities—from intelligence and toughness to passion and trust— that are essential for team success. Each expectation aligns vertically to the other qualities it impacts. This helps visualize the team-building process and identify skills and areas to improve while providing a roadmap for team success.

Every person has the potential to master all twenty-one expectations, but it takes a good facilitator with the help of an entire team to make it happen. Developing the qualities of an extreme teammate requires zero physical talent. Instead, it's about learning how to find and develop the best in yourself and then doing the same for your teammates. Best of all, the value of the Extreme Teammates framework isn't limited to short-term success with one particular team or organization. These are lessons that will translate to success throughout your life not only on teams but also in realizing personal goals and dreams. Transform your team, transform your life.

CHAPTER 1
The Power of Extreme Teammates

Being part of a team can be one of life's most powerful experiences. When people use their talents to work together, when a common goal pushes individuals towards their best selves, something special happens. Something life-changing. Being part of a team—being accountable to something bigger than ourselves—isn't easy. It's full of challenges, obstacles, and pitfalls. But when it works, it's a transformative experience. A path to greatness.

Being part of a great team is a process, an undertaking that offers lessons for the individuals on the team and for the community to which the team belongs. As an individual, a great team can help us discover our own unique talents and make us responsible to something greater than ourselves. A great team can create lifelong bonds between all of its members, regardless of their backgrounds, broadening our worlds and encouraging us to discard prejudice and bias. For a community, a great team can break down social barriers and expose us to new ideas, cultures, and concepts. A great team can be a catalyst for change, a special force that transcends society's limitations and reshapes its community for the better.

While a few core principles of teamwork have remained fairly consistent over time, others are constantly evolving and improving. The businesses, teams, and organizations that stay at the forefront of these changes will have a competitive advantage over those that don't.

When Michael Jordan and Tom Brady were in high school, nobody was predicting they would end up in the Hall of Fame, household names and legends in their lifetimes. Most people thought Jordan would go to North Carolina and sit on the bench for four years, and Brady was chosen 199th overall in the NFL draft. Both were misunderstood; both had hidden talents and strengths that went unseen. Both led their teams to astonishing achievements.

It's amazing how many young people continue to get overlooked because of size, strength, speed, test scores, or athleticism but end up proving everyone wrong. It's true that people grow, develop, and mature differently, but it begs the question: What dormant or undervalued qualities that ultimately allowed these people to achieve greatness might have been overlooked when they were young? Was it competitiveness? Work ethic? Passion? Determination? Was it a combination of several attributes? Or was it something undefinable, unquantifiable—some obscured fire burning in their hearts?

Professional scouts and college coaches will admit that one of their most significant challenges is choosing their players. It's a vexing process, and it's no secret that recruiters will leave no stone unturned in their efforts to gain insight on a player. They will look at the essentials—raw talent, potential, skills. They will study data, watch film, observe how players react to exhaustion and defeat. Scouts even attempt to get a glimpse of potentially insignificant details— things like how they tie their shoes, how they throw away a piece of trash or how they treat a stranger. Even armed with loads of information, sometimes recruiters get it right and sometimes they get it wrong. The same is true in the business world. No matter how rigorous a job application process may be, sometimes employers will choose the right candidate—the one who fits with the rest of the team and adds value to the company—and sometimes they will choose the wrong candidate.

Jacob Hester was a running back for LSU from 2004 to 2007. He wasn't the fastest, the strongest, or the most versatile athlete on the field. He looked awkward when he carried the ball. He was the kind of player who often gets overlooked. But he had an amazing career at LSU. He embodied work ethic, determination, perseverance, and passion. He had grit, toughness, and spirit, and he was a great teammate because all of those intangible qualities rubbed off on his teammates—they were better because he inspired them to be better. Major League catcher David Ross was once considered a selfish player. But he eventually saw the light, became a great teammate, and helped the Chicago Cubs win a World Series. He was essential to the team not because of his *physical* qualities but because of the unselfish and unquantifiable *mental* qualities that he inspired in his teammates.

Obviously, there isn't a foolproof system to predict the future. Some athletes peak too early; some are too mentally fragile; some are too selfish; some are too damaged; some are shackled with hidden weaknesses; and some are injury prone. The performance of even the most talented, promising athletes at the top professional programs is still vulnerable to the ups and downs of life.

However, there are two characteristics that consistently appear in every team that reaches greatness. They are mentioned in almost every Hall of Fame speech, and they are the link between great people and great teams. These two qualities, routinely undervalued and frequently overlooked, could be the best indicators of future greatness, in sports and in life—the ability to master one's mental talent and the desire to be a great teammate. This book teaches you how to do both.

Physical Talent vs. Mental Talent

Defining physical talent is simple—your speed, your strength, your ability to jump, compute, react, pursue, or throw. Physical talent improves through work and experience; this is why we practice. But the fact remains that some people are born with tons of physical talent and some are not.

Your physical talent has limits, but your mental capacity does not. Mental talent can be controlled and cultivated. Mental talent can be taught. Mental talent includes all twenty-one expectations of the Extreme Teammate Pyramid, such as trust, perseverance, competitiveness, toughness, passion, accountability, and intelligence. Mastering these areas transforms good teammates into extreme teammates. It's how people with limited physical talent find a place at the table, and it's how great athletes separate themselves from good athletes, finding a place in the Hall of Fame while those with similar talent do not.

The great news is that mental talents are inclusive—anyone can develop them. You might not be the best player, all-conference, or even a starter, but by learning how to develop your mental talents you will become an essential member of the team. More importantly, learning how to inspire, cultivate, and improve the mental talents of your teammates will give you a lasting framework for leadership that will benefit you long after sports are in the rearview mirror.

What is an extreme teammate?

An extreme teammate is any team member who takes exceptional and intentional action to assure that the success of the team comes before all things. These people may or may not have physical talent, but they have mastered their mental talent in a way that inspires and influences their teammates to be better. They have the crucial desire to be a great teammate but they also possess an obsessive commitment to achieve greatness.

Who qualifies to be an extreme teammate?

Anyone. Extreme teammates can be business leaders, coaches, custodians, CEOs, players, team managers, employees— virtually anyone who is committed to putting the team ahead of themselves. They don't need to have the most talent or the most experience, and they don't need to be appointed or assigned by someone at the top. They only need to have the drive to master their mental talent and the desire to be a great teammate and improve the people around them. Extreme teammates develop a vested interest in the growth of others because they adopt a fundamental belief that the team comes first regardless of anyone's current status, role or responsibility. If you're not there yet, don't worry; our tools will get you where you need to be.

Who should be an extreme teammate?

Everyone. When a majority of your team embraces the goal of being an extreme teammate, several things start to happen. First, your team culture is not only created but it also becomes protected and defended by the team. Second, team standards no longer get ignored; instead, teammates hold each other accountable by enforcing them. Last, disruptors such as individual goals, dishonesty, lack of trust, jealousy, selfishness, and personal agendas get drowned out by team goals, which put everyone on a mission together. People don't destroy things that belong to them.

Good Teammates vs. Extreme Teammates

You are doomed to be simply good if being good is your standard. Being good at something can become the enemy of being great at something. Good is stagnation. Good is slightly better than an average season. Good is happy with meeting the basic goals. Good is staying just ahead of the pack. Good is making a C+ on a test and being content with it. Good is slight profitability. Good is staying in your lane, not rocking the boat, and doing just a little bit better than expected. Good is doomed to third or fourth place. Good will usually miss promotions. Good is an unremarkable career. Good is often safe. Good is never great.

Bad teammates can become extreme teammates if they are willing to change and willing to learn. But, convincing good teammates to become extreme teammates can be more of a challenge because those who are simply good have often become content, complacent, and comfortable. These people usually have the capacity of a high performing extreme teammate but somehow along the way they have unintentionally been conditioned for mediocrity and are comfortably stuck being average.

The difference. Good teammates are good at inspiring themselves, but extreme teammates are great at inspiring others. Good teammates typically take their physical talent for granted while extreme teammates are always working to improve. Good teammates might listen and learn from instruction, but extreme teammates make sure everyone understands. Good teammates take responsibility for their own actions while extreme teammates promote collective responsibility. Good teammates are happy when they are playing, but extreme teammates are happy when they are winning. Good teammates put in extra work when they feel good, but extreme teammates put in extra work when they don't feel good. Good teammates follow team rules and standards, but extreme teammates are willing to enforce them. Good teammates will go along to get along while extreme teammates have the courage to speak up and tell hard truths. Good teammates ignore people that complain or criticize, but extreme teammates intervene in order to protect the team's culture. Good teammates believe that life is primarily about themselves, but extreme teammates believe that life is really about other people.

Extreme teammates bring passion, enthusiasm, and optimism to all situations. They make people believe in themselves. They demand maximum toughness, discipline, and effort. They thrive on competition, and they embrace adversity. They become selfless leaders who sacrifice personal glory for the good of the team. And their most important attribute—they know how to make other people become extreme teammates.

How would you currently score yourself as a teammate? Are you bad, good, or extreme? Do you have room for improvement? Are there things you can start doing immediately to become better? Would your team gain a competitive advantage if everyone stopped being good teammates and committed to becoming extreme teammates? The good news is that this transition is not as difficult as you might think, but it does require intentional action, a growth mindset, and a commitment to placing the success of the team ahead of yourself.

Embrace the "team-first" mindset

To begin this process, it is absolutely imperative that you condition your mind to put the team first in everything you do, everything you say, and everything you think. By fully adopting a team-first mindset you will establish the trust that is necessary between teammates to take extreme action when extreme action is needed. It will give you the courage to speak the truth to people when the truth is necessary. It will give you the wisdom to promote and defend your team culture through transparent communication. It will give you the confidence to seek new opportunities to improve yourself and to inspire those around you to improve themselves.

A team-first mindset is the foundation that will give you the leverage to be intentional in how you interact with people. If your intentions are always to put the team first, you will find that your mistakes will be accepted and even respected by your teammates. This attitude and approach will make you personally more willing to take risks and move outside of your own comfort zone to do the things that you once expected other people to do for you.

Everyone has the ability to put the team first, the potential to go from good to extreme; it's a choice that does not require physical skills or talent but rather a commitment to developing the mental capacity in everyone. Wherever you're at on the teammate spectrum, now is the time to start moving the needle. Your team depends on it, and your own future will be stronger for it. Not sure how to begin? The Seven Strategies of Extreme Teammates will get you started.

CHAPTER 2
Seven Strategies of Extreme Teammates

You always remember your mistakes. It was my first year as a varsity head basketball coach, and I was at a new school. I was facing big expectations. The previous year the team went 24-4, a glorious season, but almost all the top players had graduated. I was a new coach in a rebuilding year, but I did have a bright spot—Chris.

Chris was 6'3'' and very athletic. He was a ferocious competitor, naturally gifted, and an all-around tough and serious player, the kind of player you can build a team around. He was quiet and pleasant. He never had problems with anyone. There was something mysterious about him if you looked closely, and I suspected that Chris might have some challenging issues outside of school. But I was young and all business, and I never inquired about his personal life. I didn't care. I wanted to use him as a springboard for a good season.

A few days before our first game, I told the team they would be required to wear nice clothes to school on game day—button-down shirts, slacks, dress shoes. This is a common practice for midwestern high school basketball programs, but Chris approached me in private and explained that he didn't have any dress clothes to wear. I recognize now that just speaking to me about this took courage and wherewithal, but at the time I saw it as an obstacle that we could get around, nothing more.

So, I called my buddy Kent Niebrugge, who was about the same size as Chris and asked if he had some extra clothes for this kid. Kent was a basketball junkie like myself and lived about forty-five minutes away. He said he had plenty of clothes lying around, so I jumped in the car after practice and headed to his house.

I walked in, and Kent was digging through his rack of styles from the 90s—lots of horizontal lines, flannel shirts, and baggy cargo pants, Tommy Hilfiger, Nautica, and Ralph Lauren. Good stuff, but Kent was happy to get rid of it. By the time we were finished, he had accumulated two large bags of clothes, four pairs of dress shoes, and a couple of belts—all of it pretty nice stuff, too, considering the fashion of the era.

The next day after practice, I pulled Chris into the office to give him the clothes. He sat down and looked into the bags. He nodded his head, paused for a few seconds—I wish I knew what he had been thinking—and said, simply, "Thanks." He took the clothes back to the locker room. Everything fit perfectly, even the shoes. The next day, I overheard a teacher comment about how handsome he looked in his new clothes. I felt like I had accomplished something, done a good deed, and helped the team in the process. I was glowing with self-satisfaction.

Four games into the season we found ourselves at a respectable 2-2, not bad at all for a rebuilding year. Chris was the focus of our team, the best player on both sides of the ball. He was our leading scorer, leading rebounder, our best defender, and the dominant presence on our team.

And, thanks to Kent's generosity via my quick thinking, he had a full wardrobe of game-day clothes. It seems silly to say it now, but I thought I had saved Chris somehow. In my naive and inexperienced thinking, it appeared that we were on the right path and headed towards greatness. A winning season, perhaps the playoffs. Maybe it wasn't a rebuilding year, after all. Maybe we had a championship team on our hands. With Chris at the helm, maybe we were moving towards something rare, something special, something spectacular.

I was wrong.

Winter break came. We had an eighteen-day stretch with no school, no games, no tournaments. I had the tricky problem of keeping the team fit, hungry, and motivated during a time when most people relax, eat too much, and chill.

We planned on watching film, working on fundamentals, and doing some team-building activities. I was excited to practice during the break. Again, in my first year as head coach, I wanted to make a statement. I had big plans.

Our first practice of winter break was attended by everyone on the team. Everyone except for Chris.

I was worried. The best player on the team wasn't at practice. I asked some of the seniors about Chris. They informed me that Chris probably would not be coming to any of the winter break practices because it just seemed like too much work for him. They didn't really know why, but I accepted their version of things.

I suspected that Chris might have had some other priorities at home, especially during break, but I never inquired. I didn't go by his house. I didn't do anything other than wonder and assume.

Chris missed every practice over break. This was disappointing, but also insulting. I had done a lot for this kid—given him $500 dollars' worth of clothes, built the team around him, treated him with respect. And he bailed on the team. On me. I was furious.

To add insult to injury, once school started, Chris showed up to practice and entered the gym like nothing had happened. "Coach," he said, "I thought I would come in and scrimmage against your guys." I politely asked him to leave. He did. We went on to lose the next twenty games and finished the season 2-22.

If you think Chris failed the team or failed me, then you have drawn the wrong conclusion. I failed him. I was too focused on the end result and was never concerned with truly building a relationship with this kid. I didn't see him as a person, but simply as a means to an end. And, with my own ego in the mix, I was too worried about enforcing discipline to realize that Chris needed the team more than the team needed him. I was bitter, small-minded, and shortsighted. I was too angry to see Chris's situation as an opportunity to build a culture where teammates would fight for each other, look out for each other.

In short, I gave up on Chris. I abandoned a player on my team. And if you value your team, nobody should ever give up on anyone, ever. Sometimes the most challenging people are the ones that need us the most.

Looking back, the sting of losing twenty straight games in a row pales in comparison to the shame of giving up on Chris.

I was eventually fired, probably for losing games or maybe for not playing the preferred players; I was never told why, and it doesn't really matter now. I should have been fired for losing Chris; that would have made sense. But like me, nobody on the team or in the community appeared to be advocating for Chris.

Nobody tried to drag him back to practice, nobody went by his house or got in contact with him. Nobody ever showed him the value of commitment and accountability. Nobody displayed any concern about his well-being. Ironically, many of his teammates were actually very committed, accountable, and responsible, but as their coach I failed to inspire them to get Chris back in the program where he needed to be. They didn't see Chris as their responsibility, and neither did I.

If only I knew then what I know now.

Seven Strategies of Extreme Teammates

We're born with some talents and some we have to develop. And all the athletic talent in the world doesn't make you an effective teammate. As you work to improve your physical talent, realize that developing your mental talent is just as important, possibly more important.

When we lift up other people we lift up ourselves; when we advance other people, we advance ourselves; and when we teach other people we teach ourselves. These are axioms, universal truths, and they are the guiding wisdom of our seven strategies.

And, although they might come easier and more naturally for some people, every quality of an extreme teammate is a learned behavior.

Some of these strategies you will find easy to implement while others will take more effort to develop, but these strategies can be mastered by anyone. It doesn't take God-given talent, but it does take a willingness to modify your expectations and commit to improving the way you interact with the people on your team. Consider what you want people to say about you as a teammate in ten years, thirty years, or even fifty years. If you achieve your personal goals within the team, how do you want to be viewed by the people who were with you during that journey? The following seven strategies will have a positive impact on you and your teammates in the short term, but more importantly, by teaching you how to inspire greatness in others, they will be the foundation for all of your future successes, in sports, business, and beyond.

The first strategy of extreme teammates: Build relationships with ALL people

When people decide to work together and focus on their similarities instead of their differences, remarkable things start to happen. Significant growth occurs and amazing connections can be formed when you intentionally seek to learn about someone that is completely different than you. It's human nature to be most comfortable establishing relationships with people that are similar to us. We evolved, over millennia, to see other creatures as either predators, prey, or mates. So, it's natural to seek out people who look like us, have similar beliefs and a similar cultural background. But teams, like life, operate best when people are open, curious, and even excited by meeting new people.

Charles Barkley was great friends with an Asian American man named Lin Wang. Mr. Wang was a cat litter scientist with a PhD from the University of Iowa. They met when they were the only two people sitting in a hotel bar and they struck up a conversation. This chance encounter led to a strong friendship. Charles Barkley and Lin Wang were completely different people from different cultures and different backgrounds, but they found common interests and deep appreciation for each other through meaningful conversation. Mr. Wang recently lost his battle with cancer. Of his unlikely relationship with a star NBA player, his daughter, Shirley Wang wrote, "Barkley and my dad both worked hard—so hard, they believed, that the color of their skin didn't matter."

Think about that for a moment. A world-famous athlete was close friends with a scientist who focused on cat litter.

What's the lesson here? Is the fact that Charles Barkley befriended a Chinese American scientist from Iowa irrelevant to Barkley's success on the court? I would argue that it is quite the opposite—Barkley's openness to others is exactly one of the essential qualities that has allowed him to experience success throughout his career. Be intentional and be willing to make a great effort to get to know different people. Give yourself permission to be curious about other people—ask about their passions, their challenges, their dreams. Study up on other cultures. Be invested in finding common ground with people from other countries, people who don't look or sound like you. Take time to ask questions, be willing to answer the questions of others. Be open to the wider world.

Coaches and teams can facilitate some of this through team-building, and there are countless creative ways to make this happen. We have listed several ideas in the Appendix at the end of the book.

But, ultimately, this is a skill that you should learn to do on your own. It is crucial that you intentionally work to build better relationships with as many different people as possible. This will fast-track your growth as a person and build your capacity to solve problems with teammates of all stripes today and in the future.

The second strategy of extreme teammates: Empower everyone's talents

One of the most powerful things you can ever do for someone else is to help them find their purpose in life. To do this, you must establish the trust that is necessary for people to reveal their purpose, passion, and dreams. You have to share things about yourself to get others to share with you. You have to make yourself vulnerable. By opening up, you allow others to open up, too.

Everyone is born with gifts. We all have talents. Our gifts can translate into meaningful roles on a team if they are recognized and cultivated. Great leaders—of teams, businesses, organizations, and countries—are very good at identifying those gifts in people. This is one of the essential qualities of being a strong leader. But extreme teammates are also responsible for searching out, identifying, and empowering the gifts of others. Sometimes these gifts are obvious, and sometimes they are sitting hidden and dormant, waiting to be cultivated.

Bringing out the talent in others—and talent often walks hand in hand with passion—is something teammates can and should do.

The teammate relationship is unique. Teammates are in the trenches together. Teammates are going through common ordeals for a common cause. Teammates are in a special position to expose the individual talents of their colleagues, and they need to do this so that the overall team is stronger.

Why is this so important? When people are able to use their gifts to make their team better, they become empowered. When people become empowered, they become more willing to take ownership of the team. When ownership occurs, people become eager to enforce standards. When a team decides it's important to enforce their own standards, people get excited about sacrifice and selflessness. When people get excited about selfless sacrifice, they put the team in a position to overachieve because they are working, striving, and achieving for each other instead of for themselves. When a majority of your team takes this approach, you are on your way to creating a culture and climate that is primed for success. A collection of individuals that become something larger, a cohesive whole.

In order to have a chance at this, teammates must be willing to share their talents with each other. There is a misconception that self-improvement primarily occurs when we focus on investing in ourselves. This is false. Individual work is essential, sure, but the truth is, incredible growth occurs when we focus on investing in one another and helping others improve by utilizing and sharing our own talents.

The formula is simple. Whatever you are excellent at, whatever you do at an extremely high level—this is what you should be giving to other people. If you're great at learning new things, for example, then you are qualified to teach other people. If you are fully committed to the standards of the team, then you are qualified to enforce them. If you have an extremely good work ethic, then you are qualified to invite other people to join you in doing extra work. If you are extremely competitive, then you are qualified to encourage other people to compete at your level.

If you have good intentions, you don't need someone's approval to start leading in areas where you are already strong. If you feel like you need approval, then go get it. Essentially, if you're already an extreme teammate at something, be willing to share it.

However, before you can demand something from somebody else, you first have to master that area yourself. You can't demand the best effort of teammates unless you always give your best effort. You can't demand honesty from teammates unless you always speak with honesty. You can't demand trust from other people unless you are always trustworthy. You can't demand commitment from people unless you are fully committed. You can't demand selflessness from people unless you consistently model unselfish behavior.

Excellence is not just its own reward but its own responsibility. When you are performing at an excellent level, not only are you qualified to teach, encourage, and demand excellence from others but you are also *obligated* to make that part of your contribution to the team. If you don't find a way to give your talents, strengths, and high-level skills back to your teammates through teaching, mentoring or leadership, you're being selfish with your mental talent.

Most people don't withhold on purpose; they've been conditioned to see their own individual growth as the ultimate goal. But once you start giving more of yourself, once you start sharing your mastery, the people around you will not only listen and improve, they'll share their areas of excellence too. It becomes a kind of perpetual motion machine of group improvement, an empowerment engine.

This idea of empowerment has far-reaching consequences. If you're a coach or a leader, stop waiting for the perfect player or perfect employee to come through your system; instead, commit to building up the people you have. If you're a player, stop waiting for someone else to give you the keys to the bus; start driving it on your own with a full commitment to contributing your talents and exposing the gifts of others. If you are an employee, stop waiting for someone to expose your talents and then be disappointed when it never happens; instead, be proactive and start promoting the things you can do while also promoting the great things your co-workers can do. Be intentional. Share your skills. Impose your will on the circumstances around you instead of letting your circumstances dictate what is possible.

Learn how to give power statements. A power statement is simple, declarative, and short. It's usually exchanged by two people who have established trust, but they do not have to be friends. Often a power statement comes directly from a teammate. (I know it did for me.) A person might say something like: "I see something in you," or: "I believe in you," or: "You are a great player," or: "I know you can do this," or: "You're going to do big things."

The above are simple and straightforward, positive and effective. At some point in your life you've probably had someone say something to you that made you believe in yourself. Everyone needs to hear power statements. Everyone craves affirmation.

The ancient Romans had a saying: "Character is destiny." I believe it, but character can be molded. A person's character can be built. Self-confidence—not arrogance—leads to increased performance. Self-confidence can be grown.

So, don't wait around for someone to inspire you and believe in you. Instead, start figuring out how you can inspire someone else. When given sincerely, a power statement could be something a teammate will never forget. Think about your teammates, about what they are contributing. Think about their passions and dreams and what they might need to hear. Focus on the good, use your words, and build them up.

The third strategy of extreme teammates: Compete for everything

Competition, wanting to win, hating to lose. These inherent things should be embraced as a gift, not viewed as a flaw. A team loaded with competitors will almost always defeat a team loaded with non-competitors, regardless of the level of talent.

Competing against your own teammates or co-workers is completely natural, necessary, and encouraged. It's healthy to battle and compete against a teammate in practice and fight for playing time. It's even more healthy to go head to head against a teammate and then have the maturity to help that same teammate improve as a player or as a person. This is a selfless investment in a teammate and one of the purest ways to create a connection that will last forever.

Eliminate jealousy. Be happy for your teammates when they are successful. If you lose your starting spot, fight to get it back. Your teammates have not cheated you; they are fighting for playing time, too. This kind of competition makes for dynamic teams and hungry players. Be happy when your teammates do well. If you have a team-oriented mindset, then you are doing well, too. When you invest in your teammates, their success is a reflection on you, and, more importantly, it is a credit to the team and the organization.

It's a crucial distinction: you have to compete, but compete selflessly. You are contributing your talents to a series of collective goals, not to your own glory. Look no further than the very fine movie *Rudy* for an example. In the movie, the title character is an over-enthusiastic walk-on who is small and slow but practices hard, often irritating his teammates. One of his teammates tells him to cool it. "If I cool it," he says, "I won't be helping you get ready for the game." He contributes selflessly, knowing he'll never start and probably won't even play. He competes to help the team be stronger.

Selfish people—in sports, in life, in business—often succeed in the short term but fail over the course of a career. You have to build alliances and friendships; you have to construct something beyond your own ambitions. If you don't, your teammates and co-workers won't help you or look out for you, and you won't be able to draw upon the experiences of others to improve your own performance. Compete, yes, and be ferocious in your competitions, but do it for the betterment of the entire team. When you do this, you will become the best possible version of yourself.

The fourth strategy of extreme teammates: Make each other better

As an extreme teammate, you should always ask yourself two things: How can I help someone else get better? And, how can other people do the same for me?

Being an extreme teammate includes an intentional effort to help other people improve. You have to work, and sometimes work hard, to find ways to help your teammates. You may not always get something in return, but if you continue to give, you will also find that your teammates will contribute to your growth in return.

Here is a simple example. The most unathletic person on a sports team might be a whiz at calculus. And one of the most talented players might need help in math while the whiz at calculus might have trouble understanding new drills. Well, make the connection and form a trade-off. This can definitely involve more than two people; be creative with your trade-offs and simply search for ways your teammates can help each other achieve, on the field and off.

You need each other. This is why it is crucial that all teammates build relationships with each other, not just with the friends that they already have on a team. Everyone has needs. Everyone has gifts. Everyone has strengths, and everyone has weaknesses. So, work together. Communicate. Find ways in which people can help each other grow.

The trade-off does not always have to be equal, but it is helpful when there is a give and take mentality as it benefits the team when all parties get something. A mutually beneficial relationship is the healthiest.

Often, you'll have to be a teacher. And often you'll have to be the student. The two are linked. You'll have ample opportunities to do both.

If you learn differently—if you are a visual learner, for example—then don't be afraid to ask for a demonstration. Confusion and ambiguity are the enemies of greatness, so don't allow either into your mind. Once you understand something, then be proactive and make sure everyone else understands, too.

The fifth strategy of extreme teammates: Influence people with optimistic perseverance.

Teammates must be positive with each other, but they also have to be honest. These two imperatives are sometimes at odds with each other. It is impossible to be positive all the time, especially if there is a teammate who keeps screwing up. Don't be hard on yourself if you slip into a negative mood once in a while. You're human.

But. You must react to negative experiences, setbacks, human error, and the rest with optimism all the time. Optimism isn't a castaway notion or a silly cliché. Optimism is how people learn to persevere. Being optimistic is how people learn not to give up on anything or anyone. Bad things happen. Teams lose. People get hurt. Referees make bad calls. You lose when you should win. You make unforced errors. You cannot give into the dangerous allure of admiring the problem—where you spend more time lamenting a situation instead of trying to resolve it—and you cannot allow gloomy despair to take hold. Instead, utilize the *next play* mentality and inspire it in each other by never allowing teammates to look backwards.

Some of us tend to find problems, and some of us tend to find solutions. The world is filled with naysayers, with people who give in to failure. Be the kind of person who looks for solutions. Pessimism is contagious, but so is optimism. I've interacted with both kinds of people, and fighting alongside someone who believes in you and in the team is easier, and more fun, than butting heads with someone on your own team who believes you can't win.

If a teammate is struggling, engage them with optimism. If the team falls apart at the end of the game, go ahead and experience the bitter taste of defeat in your mouth because that taste is important, but then engage in optimistic perseverance. You'll be a better player, a better teammate, and a better person.

You'll also be happier.

The sixth strategy of extreme teammates: Take action to enforce standards

Low standards lead to weak results, failure, excuses, and defeat. They also lead to mediocrity and stifled potential. If you have standards that are high but not enforced, you'll get the exact same results: failure and defeat.

Put another way: if you let something happen, you are promoting that outcome. Think about young children. They are looking at what actually happens, not what is said or threatened or promised. If you offer a reward or consequence but never deliver, then no lessons are learned, no good behaviors are reinforced, no bad behaviors are discouraged. What you enforce is what matters. Children understand this, and you should, too.

When it comes to standards, you're one of three things: a sleeper, a promoter, or a person who takes action. The sleeper fake sleeps when something is going on so they can always say: "It's not on me." The sleeper passes the buck, looks the other way, can't be bothered. The promoter goes along with the group because they don't really have a personal set of standards. The promoter will excel if the team culture has high standards and flounder when the culture is weak. People who take action, on the other hand, know their own standards and have the courage to defend them.

Being a *take action* person isn't easy. Everyone has been in a situation when they should have done something, should have said something, should have stood up for high standards but didn't. Oftentimes it isn't a moral failing but rather a simple matter of being caught off-guard. So you have to learn how and when to intervene, how to defend the team and its values. This will sometimes lead to uncomfortable confrontations, but the stakes are the very soul of the organization.

A key idea here is the notion of cognitive dissonance. This is the mental discomfort experienced by a person who holds two or more conflicting beliefs, ideas, or values in their head at the same time. This discomfort can be triggered by a situation in which a person's beliefs clash with something new. Being on a team means being part of a society, a culture, and every society and culture has their codes, or norms. Finding fault, chastising or confronting a teammate, can feel like a violation of the team's culture, of the code of behavior that governs your interaction with your teammates. But when you see someone falling short of the team's high standards, it's time to be a person of action. Thus, the cognitive dissonance.

Former presidential candidate and CEO of Hewlett-Packard Carly Fiorina has a great approach to this. She believes that most people have good intentions, but there are always some people that are careless or clueless with the words they use. These people are usually good people deep down and often don't realize they are causing harm or being cruel. They haven't examined their actions, and they don't think through their words carefully. Most sins on a team aren't calculated; they are thoughtless. Fiorina believes that we must simply confront these thoughtless, careless, or clueless people when it is necessary, in order to keep everyone adhering to high standards, and she is correct.

If someone on the team is criticizing another player, it is your duty to put an end to it by saying something. If someone is complaining about playing time in the locker room, you should speak up and stop the person from destroying team culture. If someone is making poor decisions, it is your obligation to step in for the good of the team.

The team cannot rely on the coaches or designated leaders to do this work. The people most qualified to enforce the standards are the team members. If everything is enforced from the top down, the individual members will start bristling, resisting, and pushing back. Top-down standards lead to an unhealthy culture, one where no one is responsible for anything because everything is always someone else's fault. A good culture has agreed upon standards that everyone enforces, all the time.

Extreme teammates are leaders that take action. They have to. Do you want to be a leader or a follower? Do you want to sit by while a team erodes, or do you want to work towards something bigger? No one sets out to be a follower, and you shouldn't accept it in yourself. Adopting a plan for action and intervention will prepare you for potential problems and pitfalls. It will also train your mind for future endeavors.

Think about a mob of kids watching another kid getting bullied. You see it all the time. Some people whip out their phones and video the horrors, some laugh, some back away uneasily. Often no one intervenes. Why? For most people, it's because they are either afraid or unsure how to disrupt the violence.

I spoke with a young man after I heard he had witnessed a fight that got out of hand and had done nothing to stop it. I asked him: Why didn't you do anything? You could have stopped it easily.

He was ashamed. He shook his head and said, simply, "I didn't know how to do it. I feel terrible."

Intervening in order to maintain standards, whether on the playground, on the court, in the locker room, or in the boardroom, is almost always simply a question of doing the right thing. The right thing is rarely easy. The right thing isn't always clear. But, if you practice, prepare yourself, train your mind, and take small steps, you can do it. You can be a person who takes action, sometimes even a hero. It takes confidence and conviction, but these are things you can build in yourself and in others. The more people who are enforcing standards, the better.

If you are on a team, no matter your status, you have the ability to influence your teammates. And sometimes you'll have an obligation to take action and intervene. Don't avoid the difficult conversations. Don't look away. Don't be asleep, and don't be a sheep.

The seventh strategy of extreme teammates: Impact the lives of others

Sometimes we are reluctant to take the time to help or guide or even get to know our teammates because we think we will lose something. The truth is, impacting the lives of your teammates or of other people around you can bring unexpected rewards and exciting experiences that promote remarkable growth.

Organizational leaders, such as head coaches, CEOs, and business managers, are constantly searching for selfless people with a desire for greatness and a growth mindset. Organizational leaders are always on the hunt for extreme teammates, people who can impact others. Organizational leaders are desperately waiting for people to step up and have the courage to take action on issues within the group or organization, for people to see a need and come up with a solution.

Sometimes a coach or boss is unclear about values and expectations. Sometimes confusion makes its way through an organization because there isn't a clear vision or set of goals. This creates an environment where people are hesitant, unsure, oftentimes wavering. Unsure people are unlikely to take risks. Unsure people are unlikely to assume ownership. Who wants to be responsible for something in a system they don't understand? Sometimes teammates can't push each other because the environment is muddled, disorganized, corrupt, or mismanaged.

However, if you really desire to improve yourself as a player or advance yourself in the workplace, the single most important thing you can do *right now*, regardless of the current leadership or its expectations, is to find ways to advance and impact the people around you. If you're afraid to rock the boat, take comfort. Most organizations want to see team members improve the other people on the team. You will never be punished for helping others do their jobs better.

A bonus: being a positive presence in your teammates lives will give you immense satisfaction and make you a better person. Clemson head football coach Dabo Swinney is a great example. In 2011 he hired David Saville, a special needs young man, as his equipment manager. Saville has a job, he has a purpose, and, as a member of the Clemson team, he has a national championship ring.

But it's Swinney who has been enriched. Saville is an inspiring presence on the Clemson campus and in the football program. You could argue that Saville has made Swinney a better coach.

The extreme teammate obligation

It doesn't matter if you're the head custodian or the head coach, if you are the starting quarterback or the last person off the bench. Everyone has the potential to be an extreme teammate, and everyone has the capacity to contribute something positive towards the success of the team. Your current position, title, or status is irrelevant. Don't wait for permission from anyone in the organization to operate as an extreme teammate. Think of it as your duty. If you don't identify, develop, and contribute your skills and talents, or if you don't intentionally make an effort to improve other people, you're suppressing your own capacity to be the best that you can be.

You cannot wait for the coach to do everything. You cannot wait for someone to save you; you have to save yourself. As former head coach of the San Francisco 49ers Bill Walsh said, "At some point, the team has to take over the team."

CHAPTER 3
A Team Full of Leaders

It was the second official week of practice for a Big Ten basketball program. The seating area was dark and empty, but the court was lit up with energy and enthusiasm. Our coaching staff, about five of us, had observed many practices at the college level and even some in the NBA, but never anything like this. The session was poetry in motion, with everyone on a mission. It was loud, full of life, and riddled with optimism. Players were pushing each other outside of their comfort zone in a way that was productive and positive. Mistakes happened, but they were met only with encouragement from teammates.

The head coach was Bo Ryan; he was in command but appeared to be more of a facilitator. It seemed like everyone on the team had known each other for a long time, but we knew that was not the case. And, although there were obvious differences in athletic ability, it was impossible to determine which players were leading this team. Everyone was contributing and communicating, and players were consistently teaching each other. The players were committed to each other in a way we had never seen before.

We were mesmerized. And baffled. It was only the second week of practice. How could this team environment have been established so quickly? And, was this type of practice sustainable for an entire season? How did the team create a culture where everyone was so committed to each other? We muttered to each other. We scribbled in our notebooks. At some point, we wondered: Who is actually leading this team? Then it dawned on us, the answer was everyone.

We were witnessing a different way of running a sports program. Instead of followers with a couple of captains, we saw a group of players that challenged each other, rotating in and out of the teaching role. Everyone was involved in leading the team, and everyone was accountable. It was a miracle. The players cooperated; they moved in unison; they enjoyed their practice, and they celebrated their shared vision and collective mission. We had never seen anything like it.

The advantages of a team full of leaders

Of course, what we were seeing was a team full of leaders. They were there for each other. They were working hard, selflessly, to make each other stronger and therefore make the team stronger. The coach—he was brilliant at this—had created a culture where the players led.

It doesn't always work this way. ESPN has thousands of hours of footage of coaches being more upset about losing than the players themselves. Sometimes it isn't the players' fault. Apathy is common when players lack collective ownership and shared leadership. If the loss is someone else's fault, if the defeat is someone else's responsibility, then it's easier to shrug off.

The key is accountability. Not to a coach and not to a school, but to everyone on the team. When everyone feels part of a larger group, when the players are working for each other, when they take responsibility for each other and for themselves, then you are on the way to a team of leaders. And a team of leaders will defeat a team of followers every time.

When you create a system that emphasizes very little hierarchy in leadership, team members will become more interested in helping the people around them than impressing the people above them. The team will make its own rules, standards, and expectations. With ownership over the team's culture, the players will enforce rules, standards, and expectations, and follow them more willingly. With a collective agenda instead of a top-down agenda, morale will be stronger.

Collaborative energy is alchemical, magical. You will see players adapt their skills to fill in for injured people and look out for each other on and off the court. You will see improved stats for even lesser-skilled players, an almost eerily synchronized mindset, and a rumbling, full-throated joy in victory.

Effective facilitators inspire everyone to lead

Leadership is a language. Leadership is about creating opportunities for everyone. Leadership is about affording all stakeholders the chance to contribute to the vision. Leadership is about giving people the freedom to achieve team expectations in their own way.

Effective organizational leaders are almost always good facilitators—great at finding people's strengths and leveraging those strengths for the good of the team or business. A facilitator that values the principles of extreme teammates will create an environment where all people are expected to lead because this is what keeps people motivated, committed, and inspired. The leader still makes all the crucial decisions, drives the vision, and helps enforce expectations, but an effective facilitator will be focused on instilling a sense of ownership in every team member, demanding that team members hold each other accountable, and inspiring roles of leadership for everyone. Facilitators believe that people become empowered when leadership is driven by team members, more horizontal than vertical.

Great facilitators are extreme teammates.

Ten Leadership Strategies for Everyone

So how do we attain this worthy goal? How do we turn a team of individuals into something unified—a non-hierarchical team of leaders? This chapter will provide several strategies. And, over the next three chapters, we will explore how every member of the team can identify their leadership skills, contribute those skills to the team, and receive help from teammates in areas that need work.

One—Give everything a chance

The best way to destroy creativity, motivation, and passion is to squash the ideas of other people. Bad leaders kill ideas. Bad teammates mock innovative notions. Good leaders consider, give time and leeway, and allow ideas to play out to see if they might work. Be open to even the wildest notion.

You can practice outside your team. Read your cousin's crazy business proposal. Listen to the sales pitches at the mall or in the store. You don't have to buy anything, just train yourself to listen, ask questions, and *perceive* the possibilities.

A good question to keep in mind: What kind of boss or coach do you want to work or play for? Everyone wants a boss or coach who gives them a voice—on a team or in the workplace. Celebrate ideas—even the crazy ones. At some point, the horseless carriage, the light bulb, the airplane, the home computer were all wild imaginations of individual people. Keep that in mind.

Two— Influence with character

Good leaders don't need titles; they need integrity and character. Your title doesn't mean anything if you don't use its authority to make the team or organization better. And, not having a title shouldn't stop any team members from influencing the people around them through words, deeds, and actions.

So: promote good character by understanding your own standards and sharing them with others. Always evolve. Strive for synergy. You can impose integrity—even dignity—on an organization one interaction at a time. A person with good character can impose their integrity on the group simply by the way they lead their life.

People influence each other all the time, whether they mean to or not. We radiate good or bad energy; the people around us notice, and they respond in kind. People inspire with a strong work ethic or they distract with an apathetic attitude. Character is destiny, remember? Teams make dozens of choices every day, and each one of them matters. And whenever someone makes a positive decision, a decision that reflects good character and high standards, they are impacting their teammates for the good. This is leadership.

Three—Lead with honesty

Honesty is an essential part of any organization. Teammates must speak the truth. Truth to power. Truth to each other. Teammates must be able to express opinions, even if they are unpopular or contradict the status quo, to each other or the entire team becomes stagnant. Everyone deserves the truth.

But honesty also means being honest with ourselves. It means being open to hearing the truth—not just hearing but really *listening* to the truth. Absorbing criticism. Being open to growth.

Listen without vanity. Take the hard truth so that you can grow as a person. This can be very, very hard to do in sports, in business, and in life. From athletes to accountants, we all require self-confidence in order to succeed. If a team member's confidence is shaken, failure follows.

Sometimes, people are afraid to speak up or share an opinion. This is natural. No one wants to be vulnerable, to open themselves up to ridicule. People need to be inspired to get out of their comfort zone. People need a team culture that encourages and rewards honesty because the team needs everyone's input. The team needs leadership.

Be intentional with what you say, circumspect even, but speak up. Put yourself out there. And most important, be honest.

Four—Give credit to others

Expecting credit is dangerously close to expecting glory, and both are tied up with ego. This book is, in part, about ignoring your ego for the good of the team. If you do something marvelous, share the joy with other people on your team. You will be happier feeling the transcendent ecstasy of victory within the collective group.

Instead of expecting your accomplishments to be recognized, go out of your way to recognize the accomplishments of others.

Effective leaders always give credit to other people, and they inspire the group to give credit by modeling the behavior. If you do this correctly, it becomes ingrained in the team's culture—a circle of generosity. And it can work miracles.

Actively look for ways to commend to your teammates. Ask leading questions before you offer a solution to a problem. Lend a hand if you see someone struggling, then compliment them on their strategy, their tenacity, their willingness to accept help. If you accomplish something, think about all those who helped you get there, and give credit where credit is due. Build up your teammates' confidence by giving them opportunities to shine. You will be amazed at all the leaders that emerge when people feel that their effort, their skills, their talents are being acknowledged and celebrated.

Five—Encourage less hierarchy, not more

In the 2018-19 season, Draymond Green, playing for the Golden State Warriors, did not dress for a regular season game because of an injury. During a timeout, Coach Steve Kerr drew up a play and showed it to Green, who nodded his head, then led the huddle and showed the play to the team. It was a remarkable moment that at the time went unnoticed.

It would have been easier for Kerr to show the play to the team himself, so why did he make Green the middleman? Why take the extra time or the risk that something might be lost in translation. Consider the message Kerr sent with this simple gesture, the culture he was establishing. Kerr—in the middle of a game!—gave up some of his control to the team. He radiated trust and generosity. By handing the reins over to Green, Kerr modeled exactly how to share credit and build up leaders.

But there's more. Although injured, Green was still able to contribute to the team effort, and Kerr had the chance to lay some groundwork for Green's future. Kerr showed Green that he believed in him. Maybe Green wants to coach his own team someday. If you're a CEO, head coach, or team leader, find ways to give your team more responsibility—you will be rewarded many times over.

Great leadership is not about having as much control as possible. Great leadership is not about imposing your will on people. Great leadership *is* about giving away as much control as possible. When done well, the act of giving away power will not only allow your team to meet expectations, but it will often lead them to far exceed your expectations. Most people want to be given opportunities to do their best work, to shine. A great leader or facilitator is an extreme teammate who does not worry about getting the credit for victory or success or a simple job well done, but instead looks for ways to maximize the talents and skills of every team member. They believe bold ideas are stronger than hierarchy.

Why don't more coaches or leaders do this? Some don't want to give up their power. In fact, some coaches become coaches because somewhere deep inside, they enjoy the power of being able to make people work. But others, I believe, were raised in an environment where the coach or parent or boss was the divine voice, the final say. And still others aren't sure how to begin turning authority over to the players. It can feel like a chicken and egg problem.

It isn't always easy to hand over the reins, to cede control, to give up the driver's seat. There's risk. But without risk, of course, there is no reward. The key is to determine your expectations and find the right people to execute those expectations. Little by little, create small and meaningful leadership roles and give ownership of various parts of the program to people that can handle it. This will promote a change in culture that makes the team accountable to each other.

Author Simon Sinek captured it best: "A star wants to see themselves rise to the top. A leader wants to see those around them become the stars."

Six—Work hard for those around you, not above you

Forget about the boss or coach—work for your teammates' approval. Your teammates are the ones in the trenches with you, scrapping it out with you, weathering the storms with you. They are the ones who understand what you are going through. People who work primarily to impress their boss, athletes who play primarily for their coach's approval—let's be honest, there are a lot of them—live in a selfish world. They often strive for success in a variety of underhanded ways, often alienating and irritating their teammates in the process.

The animating energy of a team is and should be camaraderie—the thrill of pursuing victory, the joy of the game itself, and the rush of being part of something bigger than yourself. At best, self-promoting people detract from this, at worst, they destroy it. They are naysayers. They are often aloof, or worse, dishonest. They avoid the tough challenges to protect themselves. They play politics with the organization's leaders and with their teammates.

So, what do you do with someone on your team who is only looking out for number one? Well, if you have established trust and built a relationship with everyone on your team, you can share your thoughts with dignity. Be clear that you are looking out not just for the team, but for their reputation and their future. Ultimately, move forward by modeling—work hard to impress your teammates. Integrity is contagious.

Seven—Take ownership of something

Everyone must assume ownership and leadership in some capacity. No one can exclusively follow.

Every team, whether in sports or in industry, has dozens of jobs, roles, responsibilities to carry out. There is no reason for all of these to be in the hands of a coach and two captains. Scouting new talent? Gathering equipment? Studying the opposition? Even extra practices, workout sessions, and the like can be facilitated by any rank and file member of a team.

Bobby and Anthony were committed members of their high school basketball team. They worked hard at everything, especially physical conditioning. They pushed themselves like few players I've coached. They tried to beat their best times; they tried to win every sprint; they hit the weights like the very devil.

So the coaching staff made a decision. We met with Bobby and Anthony and asked if they could lead the team in conditioning at the end of practice each day. They seemed excited about the opportunity. We explained our expectations clearly and told Bobby and Anthony to take a day to formulate some ideas and meet with us again to share their thoughts before the next practice.

Their planning blew us away. They had researched how to combine cardio and resistance training. They even learned the science behind everything. We gave them the final ten minutes of practice.

We were shocked at what happened next, but we shouldn't have been. Bobby and Anthony took conditioning to another level. The training was harder, more inspirational, more multifaceted, and better facilitated than any workouts the coaches had put together. They also demonstrated to the rest of the team the importance of planning, the possibility that players could be leaders, and how the two always go together.

After that, Bobby and Anthony led this part of practice every day. This created authentic player leadership and ownership, and we coaches were freed up to focus on other things.

The story of Bobby and Anthony doesn't end there. We met with them to compliment their leadership, and we asked them to help us expand this experiment. We suggested that once a week Bobby and Anthony could choose two players to lead conditioning for the last ten minutes of practice. They immediately recommended two players. Since Bobby and Anthony already had ownership of this part of practice they, more than anyone, wanted to make sure that the expectations were met. So Bobby and Anthony met with the two other players outside of practice and made sure they were prepared to take on this leadership role. Bobby and Anthony transferred their preparation and resultant power to the new players.

Amazing and simple, and it worked: a chain effect of ownership took hold. The players trusted each other. They worked harder for each other. Everyone was positive. Everyone was encouraging. No one slacked off. We had replicated that magical atmosphere I described at the beginning of the chapter.

Now imagine expanding our experiment to every area of your organization, giving each member of the team some type of leadership role. Would this change your culture? Would team members be accountable to each other? Would they start performing for each other instead of working only for themselves?

Of course, the answer to all of the above is an emphatic yes. Everyone has the potential to lead, and everyone is obligated to cultivate the leadership potential of their teammates.

When this amazing cycle gets rolling, the team will witness a culture of leadership that spreads like wildfire. Everyone will want to contribute. Everyone will share responsibility. People will no longer just be leading, they will be building capacity for leadership in everyone around them. They will be paving the way for the future.

Eight—Inspire greatness in each other

No one sets out to be a follower. Parents don't enroll their children in sports programs hoping they'll develop the skills to follow other people. We don't send kids off to college hoping they learn how to be a dutiful subordinate. Yet in practice we are often willing to defer to coaches, captains, team leaders, bosses—to cede all leadership duties to a few authority figures. Why?

I think the answer is twofold. I think many of us have a natural tendency, perhaps cultivated in our earliest years, to conform, to blend in, to go along to get along. More often than not, it's easier to follow than it is to lead. And when it comes to sports, this instinct for following is exacerbated by a sports culture that has long been steeped in a kind of military mentality. Top-down; sir, yes, sir; do as your told; don't ask questions; because I'm the boss, and so on.

For years, we have been conditioned to follow a system—in school, in sports, and in the workplace—that assigns leadership responsibility to a select few. The negative effects of this system reverberate throughout an organization. On an individual level, it serves to suppress leadership capabilities, and hidden talents fail to appear. People become uninspired, underutilized, and disinterested, and they funnel their ambition into selfish advancement.

Without the drive to innovate or the friction of disagreement that arises when team members are passionate, inspired, and involved, organizations become stagnant. Divisions within the team become acceptable. Factions appear. Healthy competition is replaced with unhealthy resentment, sabotage, even cruelty. I've seen this happen in professional sports teams, in public schools, and in the workplace. It's dispiriting and, in many ways, predictable because the only way for the top-down system to yield results, you need the absolute best at the top—the most brilliant, the most talented, the most tactical leaders available. But there are many more organizations in need of leadership than there are top 1 percent leaders to lead them.

In sports, we often put unrealistic expectations on team captains. We assume they will lead with very little guidance. I've seen it. Captains are supposed to rise to every challenge, enforce standards, facilitate communication, be above petty squabbles, win championships. And, weirdly, the captains are often the best all-around athletes on a team, as if winning the genetic lottery also means you have what it takes to do the rest.

Some people can handle these expectations. Every generation has a handful of elite athletes who are also superb leaders, but these are the exception, not the rule. Shared leadership doesn't take away the responsibility of captains, it simply lessens the burden on one player by increasing expectations for every other player. Think of it as a way of training the entire team to be able to step up when needed.

Don't get me wrong, teams and organizations will always need that one person to be in charge as a facilitator—the head coach, the president, the school principal, the CEO. But within the organization, it is healthy and important for leadership and responsibility to be shared as much as possible.

Let me put it another way: a team full of followers with a few leaders is a formula for mediocrity. A team full of leaders is a formula for greatness.

Nine—Be an angel leader

A team's angel leader is similar to a charitable organization's anonymous donor. Angel leaders inspire great things while seeking no recognition or credit for themselves. An angel leader is selfless, and it takes a remarkable amount of self-confidence, and belief in the team, to become one.

I will often begin the season with a strategy that came from UNC basketball coach Roy Williams—for the first week of practice, I ask players to memorize a quote each day before we begin. A favorite: "It's amazing what can be accomplished when nobody cares who gets the credit."

I also speak to my players about being an angel leader, about being the behind-the-scenes person who does things for their teammates without ever expecting acknowledgement or anything in return.

About midway through the season, I will sometimes mail a simple motivational handout to the players, without a return address. These days, receiving actual mail is rare enough to be exciting, and I figure it is one less piece of paper to end up in a wad at the bottom of a duffel bag.

One year, a few weeks after I had mailed the letter home, a player who had been struggling with his shooting approached me before practice and said, "Thanks, coach."

"For what?"

"For putting that envelope on my bag yesterday. With the Muhammad Ali quotes."

I was shocked. And proud. I hadn't given him that envelope; one of his teammates had.

Yes, a high school kid had the selfless maturity to do this for a teammate, anonymously. People will do amazing things for each other if facilitators make angel leadership a team value by explicitly introducing the concept and by modeling a quiet, dogged, selfless commitment to others.

Ten—Find value in people

One of the most powerful characteristics of any leader is the ability to find value in people. These leaders understand that everyone deserves a voice in the organization, and they support a platform that allows everyone to be heard. Effective leaders are not threatened by relinquishing their leadership because transferring leadership doesn't equate to removing power. They encourage growth by inspiring people to take as much leadership responsibility as possible. They create chemistry by combining people's physical and mental talents.

I had a conversation with a man who owned a strong and growing company, which is all well and good, but this person was adamant that nobody else in the world could sell as well as him. He was arrogant and, in his arrogance, wasn't seeing the bigger picture of his own company.

Even if he were the best salesman on the planet and nobody could touch him, he still needed to look for ways to strengthen the rest of his team, to find value in his people.

He could have remained the primary seller, but he should have surrounded himself with a team, looked for each team member's unique talent and skills, and nurtured their potential. He would have recognized, eventually, aspects of the work that could be shared, teammates who could be trusted, and areas for his own growth. His business also would also have reaped the benefits of a team of leaders—each one striving for the greatness that he felt he had already achieved. Instead, he was busy admiring his own abilities, and, in the process, severely limiting his company's potential.

Everyone has something to contribute. Find and grow the value in your teammates and watch everyone—you, your teammates, and your organization as a whole—flourish.

Leading together

Every great team has the following things in common: A foundation of trust that is built on relationships; clearly defined roles where everyone can excel; standards and expectations that are enforced by everyone, not just select leaders; teammates who are accountable to each other; a mission that is stronger than any one person; and, most important, a culture of ownership, where all teammates are responsible for sharing their strengths, working on their weaknesses, and finding ways to improve the lives of others on the team.

So, how can you make all of this a reality? If you're a player, advocate for yourself. Find places where you can lead; show your coach what you can bring to the team. If you're an employee, advocate for yourself. Think about where your talents could be better utilized to add value to your organization; communicate to management what you can bring to the team. Learning how to advocate for yourself will teach you how to advocate for others. Step outside your comfort zone; search for opportunities and be intentional about becoming a leader in some meaningful area. Take things on. Look for problems; come up with creative solutions.

As legendary Tennessee women's basketball coach Pat Summitt said: "In order to grow, you must accept new responsibilities, no matter how uncertain you may feel or how unprepared you are to deal with them."

Everyone must find their path, their role, their contribution to the team. Don't sit back; don't be a statue—you know what birds do to statues. Don't let others make decisions for you. Don't accept mediocrity in yourself or in others. If you can contribute more to the team, then do so.

If you are a coach or manager, know that making a team full of leaders is about finding the value in every single team member. It's about unlearning some of our old assumptions about leadership. It's about grooming all your team members to become leaders, coaches and teachers. Be a great facilitator; have the confidence to relinquish control and create ownership opportunities that allow for everyone's best attributes to shine. Empower the team instead of using your power over them. Model selflessness in all that you do.

For all of us, from novice players to CEOs, the goal is to create a culture that inspires team members to be unselfish, bound by relationships, focused on a mission, and ultimately more devoted to the success of the team than to the pursuit of personal glory.

This way lies victory. This way lies greatness.

University of Minnesota head football coach P. J. Fleck puts it like this: "On bad teams, no one leads. On average teams, coaches lead. But on elite teams, players lead."

CHAPTER 4
The Foundation for Success

For every leader who intuitively knows how to bring out the extreme teammate in each member of the team, there are dozens of the rest of us out there—people who want to inspire others to greatness but just aren't sure where to begin. The Extreme Teammate Pyramid—twenty-one attributes that show us exactly what mental talents we need to develop in our team in order to achieve greatness—is where we begin.

Twenty-one may sound like a daunting number, but the good news is, if you look hard enough, your team probably has many members who have already mastered some of the twenty-one qualities or expectations of extreme teammates. Actually, every single person on the team must identify at least one area that they believe to be a strength. The qualities you identify as areas of strength or mastery are what you should be offering to your teammates. If you like teaching people, then take ownership of *application* and be responsible for creating a team full of learners, mentors, and teachers. If you naturally have a positive attitude, take ownership of *enthusiasm* and be the person that inspires a positive spirit in everyone.

Your mental talents are your gifts, and they are gifts that can easily be shared. When each member of the team is sharing their gifts, your team will have a successful and memorable experience that's filled with monumental growth regardless of physical talent.

Remember—everyone has the potential to learn, improve, and master each expectation in the Extreme Teammate Pyramid, found on page 114. And, when all twenty-one expectations are being mastered and shared between individuals, team greatness will follow. It's a lofty goal, but everyone can do it.

Establish the foundation

Everything begins as an idea: houses, businesses, sports teams, philosophies. And every idea, when put into practice, has to be planned, structured, built.

When you build a house, you lay the foundation first. So it is and so it has always been. Without a strong foundation, your house, your government, your team—no matter how strong or good-looking—will crumble.

Organizations are like houses. Sports teams and businesses have to lay a foundation before they can build anything else. The foundation of any team is its culture. And you can't have a successful and sustainable culture without first establishing three essential qualities: wellness, character, and trust.

These three items are the foundation, the pillars, and the bedrock for every great team. Without them you might have occasional victories, but you will have no long-term success. These qualities are non-negotiable. Let me say it a second time: without wellness and character and trust, your team *will fail*.

And they need to happen at the beginning. If you try to establish a foundational culture once your team's work is already underway, your team will falter; everyone will feel confused and exhausted.

Wellness, character, and trust must be established early, and they must be protected by the team.

WELLNESS
Makes wise choices. Achieves balance and joy from exercise, nutrition, education, rest and quality time with teammates, family and friends. Is thankful and forgiving. Impacts people with generosity and service.

Wellness is at the top of the Extreme Teammates Pyramid, and for good reason. Wellness is a deep set of interconnected ideas, encompassing the choices we make, the food we eat, the habits we cultivate, the attitudes we carry. Wellness also involves our capacities for love, joy, forgiveness, sacrifice, and generosity. Master wellness in the formation of a team, and watch your team members become happier, more productive people.

Put simply: We become what we are becoming. We are the choices we make. We are the habits we cultivate. So a good team will promote wellness in all of its daily activities.

We can begin with ourselves. Examine your choices. Are they impacting your mental and physical health? Are your choices restricting you or setting you free? Are they stopping you from achieving your goals or helping you attain them? Are your choices honest and noble and good for the team? And how are you influencing other people through the choices that you make? Are you looking out for others? Are you generous with your time? Are you keeping the good of the team ahead of your own ego? Are you safeguarding your mind? Are you pursuing wisdom? Are you making other people well?

In order to master wellness, you must be selective about the people you associate with and the environment you keep because these two things will either move you and your team closer to greatness or further away from it. Wellness might not look exactly the same from one person to the next. Having balance and harmony is different for everyone. Some people thrive working fourteen-hour days, some don't. Some people respond to direct criticism, others need positive guidance and support. Some people need some time alone, while others require company.

If wellness is lacking—if your team culture doesn't promote wisdom and generosity—then the people on your team will have minimal growth in all of the expectations that follow—including confidence, trust, passion, and commitment. If you aren't getting wellness right, you are, in essence, a sick organization.

However, if wellness is established early, if it is strong and thriving, then your team will have vast opportunities for physical, emotional, and intellectual improvement. Wellness isn't just about decisions made at practice, during the workday, on the field, or at the big presentation. Wellness is an idea that encompasses all the choices we make throughout our tenure on a team.

Being part of something that is bigger than ourselves carries great responsibility. Even personal decisions can affect the team. But many people miss this crucial truth and fail to understand the long term, reverberating effects of their poor choices. I knew a basketball player back in college who was a solid athlete, a power forward who, when he was motivated, was a dominating player. He also drank, like a lot of college kids, but he drank too much and often. One night during the season, he got alcohol poisoning and had to be taken to the hospital. Two of his teammates took him. They stayed up most of the night as he got his stomach pumped even though they had a big game less than twenty-four hours later. They were good teammates. He wasn't.

I don't know if they confronted him about his drinking. It isn't uncommon for people to remain silent when their teammates exhibit self-destructive behavior. But staying silent is wrong. Staying silent makes the teammates complicit. Staying silent enables the problem and harms the capacity for trust. Dishonesty, in any form—including staying silent or withholding the truth— will impact trust and it will keep your team from succeeding.

Everyone is responsible for cultivating wellness in every team member. Extreme teammates speak up. When necessary, they confront. People have to understand—or be made to understand— how their actions and choices impact others.

This isn't always easy. But if the teammate situates the advice within the team's culture and a mutual desire for success, people can learn, they can modify their behavior. Greatness is composed of a million seemingly insignificant decisions. And every decision matters.

Consider the teammate who is quick-tempered. Every team has one. A player who loses his temper, yells at the ref, screams at the coach, fouls an opponent out of anger. This kind of short-fused rager often hurts the team with these outbursts. Look no further than Zinedine Zidane, one of the greatest soccer players of all time. In the 2006 World Cup final, Zidane headbutted an Italian defender and was ejected from the game. He lost his cool and cost

France the world championship. An extreme teammate would have confronted this kind of behavior before the championship game.

The team can be a great place for individuals to grow or a place that stifles or chokes any kind of individual advancement. Teammates can sit by and watch self-destructive behavior, but this strategy of silence will ultimately punish the entire team.

Wellness is maintained through trust. Trust rests on character.

Don't be afraid to be happy

Extreme teammates know how to use gratitude and forgiveness as competitive advantages. Both are powerful forces for good in the world. Both are often overlooked.

Being thankful helps you keep your focus and your perspective. It's nearly impossible to be angry, nervous, jealous, or selfish while you are being thankful. This is why during the last two minutes of a competitive game, a great coach might say something like: "We love close games, and we are thankful that we have a chance to rise above our expectations and exceed our capacity as a team." This puts players in a grateful frame of mind and suppresses stress. Extreme teammates do this with each other; they use thankfulness as a weapon because when people truly appreciate everything they have, they actually gain a competitive advantage.

Forgiveness is equally important. Don't hold grudges against opponents, coaches, managers, bosses, teammates, or referees; it's useless and counterproductive to turn a match, a project, a meeting, or even a whole career into a tally of personal slights.

Let it go, all of it. "The weak can never forgive," Mahatma Gandhi said. "Forgiveness is the attribute of the strong."

Be thankful and don't harbor anger or resentment—these are two important steps towards happiness.

Happiness is a choice. Ask yourself a simple question: do you really believe you'll perform better if you're miserable?

Commit to supporting a greater purpose

The great Jackie Robinson said, "A life is not important except in the impact it has on other lives." A great way to build up a team's culture is to marble some kind of service—volunteering at a local homeless shelter, food pantry, or senior center, for example—into the team's routine. Everyone wants to be part of things that matter. Everyone wants to make a difference. Condition yourself to look for ways that you and your team can impact the lives of others.

Acts of service cannot be isolated. I once witnessed a group of high school players read children's books to second graders, then return to their own school and act like jerks to their classmates. I was shocked. No one had connected their volunteering to their regular lives. The players were disconnected from their own service.

Service to others must be directly connected to the team's mission. It's nice to read to young children, but the team needs to see their generosity as an extension of the team's culture and values. What matters is that the good works should start with people, not money or causes. The acts of service should be connected to the team's character—to their ability to be thankful, to how much they trust each other. The acts of service should be an outgrowth of the team's overall wellness. Then, and only then, will the impact of their service be felt both in the world and within the team.

When a team rallies around a greater purpose and works together for a cause, they are putting the very essence of the team itself—a group of individuals united for a larger goal, a higher good—to work in the world. This is how children become adults and ordinary, decent people become heroes.

CHARACTER
Acts with self-control, civility, humility, and professionalism. Influences others with honor and integrity and stands up for what is right. Contributes to humanity with kindness, compassion, and courage.

Heraclitus, a Greek philosopher, said that character is destiny. Our future isn't fixed or mapped out for us; we choose who we are, and character is the foundation for everything we do.

Recruiters, scouts, managers, and hiring directors typically place a high value on character. God-given talent is important, but talent is a gift that is temporary; character lasts forever. Character can be challenging to measure but not impossible. This is why people perform reference checks.

Character partners with wellness because we are a collection of the decisions and choices we make on a daily basis. Whether you realize it or not, character is revealed by every decision you make. Your inner self, your values and your beliefs, are revealed by how hard you work or practice, how you speak to others, what you allow, what you accept, what you defend, what you protect, and what you speak up against. Know this.

Wellness is maintained through trust. Trust rests on character. They form an essential mini-pyramid in the larger scheme.

Character is influence. You can't demand humility and empathy from your teammates, but you can definitely influence them with it. The same is true for sportsmanship and professionalism; your character can shape the entire team.

Character is crucial. A successful culture takes root in the good character of its people. It doesn't matter how high-minded or virtuous you are, you cannot create a good culture from bad character.

A team can nudge the weak character of a few individual members if a culture is already established. Think about teams like the New England Patriots that can easily absorb a gifted athlete who might have made some poor decisions. The Patriot's culture is extremely strong, and they have figured out that character is a learned behavior, and that people can change.

Character is the essence of who you are. Do you bend at pressure? Do you stand up for your convictions? Does your integrity influence and/or impact other people? Are you comfortable with your own integrity? Do you defend the defenseless? Do you do the work in front of you, even when you don't want to? Do you look for the good in other people?

Character is *not* the same thing as physical talent or skill or intelligence. There have been, through the ages, unfortunate multitudes of star athletes, successful business people, prominent politicians, etc. who have talent but lack character. I could point to numerous examples but you can pick up a newspaper on any given day and find a dozen before you get past the front page. I will instead say just this: talent without character will go underutilized.

Character is action. Words matter, sure, but it is your actions that show your true character. Posters in a school hallway about stopping bullying *do not* stop bullying; bullying only stops when people with character step up and do something.

Surround yourself with people of character. Populate your team with people of integrity. This is sound advice for your sports team, your business, and your life.

TRUST
Has faith in the program and believes in the process. Uses honesty and love to create a system of loyalty, trust and pride. Builds relationships, forms friendships and instills bonds between all people.

Sometimes it's the small things that matter—a hug, a smile, a card.

We had a big holiday basketball tournament, three games in three consecutive nights. We had a decent team but things weren't clicking. Roles were still being established. Rotations were still being determined. We were still tinkering. The players knew each other and some of them were friends, but we weren't a team yet, not really. Something was missing.

On the first night of the tournament we were on the team bus and Tony got a phone call. Tony was one of our best inside players, a real tough competitor. The phone call was terrible news; his uncle had just passed away. Tony was upset, distraught. His parents told him he would catch a flight the following evening for the funeral. He would be gone a week.

We arrived at the school. The players did their pre-game rituals and got dressed. We warmed up. I kept my eye on Tony. He seemed okay. Right before the game started, I extended my condolences and gave him a hug. "You okay?" I asked. He nodded.

After the game, we all piled back on the bus. Tony sat in the back. I decided I would get a team card later that night and have everyone sign it the next day. A small thing, but I didn't know what else to do. A couple of guys in the front of the bus asked if Tony was doing okay. The word came back that he wasn't. Before I could make any suggestions, a few players said, "Coach, we got it all figured out. Since Tony is leaving after the game tomorrow, we're going to pick up a card and have everyone come in early and sign it before we get on the bus tomorrow night."

Now, in the past, we had talked about selfless sacrifice for each other; we had talked about building relationships and creating bonds between everyone on the team; we had talked about being honest and showing love towards one another. But as a coach or a teacher, often you're not entirely sure that your works are really being heard, let alone sinking in and resonating. It's hard to know what is getting through.

When a moment arises that demands the kind of trust you have tried to instill, then you'll know. I didn't need to tell my players how to take care of their teammate. They had already figured it out. This is selfless leadership built on trust.

The next day, Tony played, but he competed with a blank stare on his face. We won the game. When we returned to the locker room, I told the team: "I am so impressed with you guys; you're more than just good players, you're great people." Tony's teammates gave him the card. He was in tears. We all were in tears because everyone in that room was with Tony, and he knew it.

The smallest gesture—a two dollar card passed from teammate to teammate to scrawl a few kind words—turned out to be the glue that bound our team together. We finished with a remarkable season, overachieved as a group and handily defeated a team that featured future NBA player Brandon Paul, a team that, based on athletic prowess alone, we had no business beating.

From that day forward, I realized that getting team members to find their own solutions not just for their own problems but for their teammates' problems, as well, is the secret sauce to creating trust. I might have had a very small part in facilitating it by helping to establish a team culture that valued strong relationships, but when it came time for action, the team took care of the team. The team took care of someone in distress; the team created bonds that would last a lifetime; the team took ownership; the team led itself. The team showed love, and love builds trust.

Love is not just a four-letter word

Love can be a tough word to use in a competitive environment, whether on the field or in the boardroom. It's a word that has been mangled by fifty years of Valentine's cards, cheesy hearts, and cornball roses. Love is often portrayed as weak or childish. It's neither. Love is the very essence of life. Love is doing what is best for others without regard for oneself.

Love in the context of a team is mutual care and understanding, a deep and abiding bond of affection. This bond gets you through the tough times, the shallows of a season or experience. Without it, teams turn on themselves, resorting to bickering, resentment, and recrimination. Without the bonds of love, a team is just a group of people who spend a little time together. And who, really, would ever define a team like that?

Great teammates show love and expect it from others. John Wooden is considered one of the greatest sports minds of all time. One of his proteges is Sue Enquist, an eleven-time national champion women's softball coach at UCLA. Wooden created the infamous leadership pyramid that many coaches and leaders have used throughout the years. I had a long conversation with Sue, and she explained that during Coach Wooden's later years, he told Sue that he regretted leaving two characteristics off his pyramid: balance and *love*. He knew that love, the often invisible connective tissue between people, was the glue that held so many great teams together.

Love doesn't happen overnight. It involves trust, and trust requires vulnerability. It can't be taken; it has to be *given*. It has to be extended. It has to be applied. But you cannot love someone if you don't trust them, and you can't trust them if you don't know them.

The gist of it is this: the relationships between your teammates matter. You could argue that the team's superficial goals—competing, completing, winning, succeeding—is secondary to the relationships. It's the relationships between team members that fuel our passion to work successfully as a team. Relationships are the very stuff of life and, therefore, the very essence of competition and success. Being an extreme teammate requires good relationships. Good relationships require honesty and trust.

Don't misunderstand. Some people are not worthy of trust. Trust is a two-way relationship that needs to be built. Over-trusting, especially the wrong people, can be just as damaging as under-trusting. Both can derail the team-building process. The best approach is to be patient and deliberate. Get your systems set up, make sure the wellness component is present and understood, and be willing to offer trust when it is time and to expect trust from others in turn.

There are always outside forces that can discourage relationship building and trust, but don't let them discourage the team. Social media should not be a replacement for conversations and relationships; use it to develop and support relationships that have already been established. Don't allow peer pressure, destructive behaviors, racial fears, dishonesty, and personal agendas to disrupt the process that creates trust between people.

Avoid tribal thinking, tribal behavior. People have the most to learn from people that are different from them.

Once relationships are created, everyone should be willing to tell each other the truth when the truth is necessary. The truth can hurt. A lot of people don't want to hear it, but the truth is vital. Usually those who can't take the truth won't be successful in a competitive environment. Everyone on the team, at a minimum, should have at least one person who will always give them the hard, unvarnished truth. Part of growth is awareness, and part of awareness is pain. Accept this, be open to it, and even expect it.

Extreme teammates tell the truth to their teammates because they are wise enough to know that even if it hurts in the short term it is the best thing for the team in the long run. It takes courage to speak the truth. You risk offending; you risk damaging a relationship. But this is a crucial point: a teammate is more than just a friend. It is a simpler, yet deeper bond. Difficult discussions are essential to the team's success. One conversation can change a teammate's life. Don't sidestep, don't be evasive, don't procrastinate. Speak the truth. Your teammate is worth it.

CHAPTER 5
Seven Attributes of Great Culture

A team culture is established when the team's expectations are ingrained in the behaviors of its members. Culture is the element that allows your team and its people to grow, develop, and flourish. Culture can be divided into seven expectations: responsibility, commitment, passion, communication, accountability, work ethic, and motivation. The culture your team has *right now* is established by the current behavior of your team members.

These seven expectations rest on a number of questions.

Who enforces your standards? Who takes ownership in how things are done within your organization? Who provides the long-term vision and goals? How do you correct damaging behavior? How do you motivate the unmotivated?

A great culture is not created by only a handful of people. A great culture is not created with a top-down structure. A great culture is not created by a captain and a coach attempting to enforce standards. A great culture is created and sustained when *everyone* takes the responsibility to enforce the standards and expectations that are important to the team.

The good news is that, with the correct framework, guidance, and leadership, anyone has the capacity to master the essential components of a great team culture—responsibility, commitment, passion, communication, accountability, work ethic, and motivation.

The first step: all expectations must be clearly communicated to everyone on the team, revisited routinely through some form of assessment, and enforced equally by everyone.

Now, many people think that you can create a great culture by placing a premium value on success, but this isn't true. Success is important, of course, it is the effect, not the cause. Strive only for the end result, for the win, without first establishing a rock-solid culture, and you will find that success is elusive and/or fleeting. Establish a great team culture, and you will discover that success naturally follows. A lot of mediocre leaders get this backwards, assuming that winning with talent alone will somehow create a culture of success. It won't. It can't. Winning is not a behavior or a skill. Success is not a team culture. Winning consistently—or losing consistently—is part of your climate.

Your team's culture informs your team's climate. For example, confidence is not culture, it's part of your climate. You can build confidence through a strong work ethic and preparation, but outside forces can deform a person's confidence. Like the weather, a person's confidence can change. But with a strong, well-established culture, over time all of the team members will become more confident. With increased confidence, you will see more ownership and motivation. And more winning.

An extreme example is Michael Jordan's infamous "flu game" in the 1997 NBA finals. Jordan and the rest of the Chicago Bulls obviously had a peerless team culture—unbelievable work ethic and unparalleled passion and motivation, but, stricken by a sudden, flu-like illness, Jordan's personal climate, his competitiveness, effort, and perseverance, were challenged. Jordan played through his illness, scored thirty-eight points, and the Bulls won. Climate can and will fluctuate due to circumstances beyond anyone's control, but with a strong culture, your team members will rise above whatever the shifting winds throw their way.

RESPONSIBILITY
Is prompt and reliable. Does not blame others or tolerate excuses. Promotes collective responsibility and shares leadership duties with the team. Influences teammates by modeling responsibility.

Pat Summit, one of the most successful basketball coaches in history, said, "You can't pick and choose the days you feel like being responsible. It's not something that disappears when you're tired."

The most basic things—being prompt and reliable—are a reflection of character and commitment. If you are naturally inclined to be responsible, then take ownership of this expectation and make an intentional effort to create an environment of collective responsibility. Extreme teammates make sure other people are on time. Practices and meetings are finite, losing time, even a few minutes, waiting for people to show up is harmful to the team and eventually results in a significant loss of productivity. Promptness is a simple behavior that is essential to creating a strong culture.

Communicate. Don't wait for others to enforce the standards. Extreme teammates let people know if they are screwing up. They approach this by letting tardy teammates know that they are important, that they are needed, on time. Extreme teammates give reminders. They set up a shared online calendar. They make a phone call or send a text. Never give up on a teammate, even if they have given up on you.

Don't take excuses. Excuses are for losers. It might sound harsh, but it's true. In sports, if your team learns how to make excuses for being late, they will learn how to make excuses for losing a game. When they learn how to make excuses for losing a game, they will learn how to make excuses for a poor season. When people create the destructive habit of making excuses, which often takes the form of blaming other people, they will learn how to make excuses for anything and everything, to blame everything on everyone else, which is a prescription for failure, in school, in sports, in business, and in life. Former football star and motivational speaker Inky Johnson says, "If the reason is not big enough the excuse will be."

Parents, listen up: when you blame others for your kids' struggles—teachers, friends, coaches, refs, teammates, conditions—you aren't building confidence, you are creating an illusion that everything in life is somehow decided by forces beyond anyone's control. University of Connecticut women's basketball coach Geno Auriemma, who has won more D1 women's championships than anyone, said that, in essence, when a player is a bad teammate, it can be traced back to her parents. That might sound grim and defeatist, but the key is this: if being a bad teammate involves behavior that was learned from our parents, then we can unlearn the bad behavior and learn how to become great teammates. It's never too late to take responsibility for ourselves.

Blaming others allows the human mind to avoid tackling challenges or asking hard questions. Making excuses is a bad habit, an insidious and particularly nasty bad habit, an emotional drain that creeps into a team and over time gradually destroys team culture. Look inward, first and always. Excuse-making is a form of selfishness, protecting the ego at all costs. Never allow selfishness to haunt your team.

Successful people refuse to rely on excuses. They are usually too focused on what needs to be done. Tiger Woods is one of the greatest golfers of all time, in part because he never makes excuses professionally or personally.

We can learn to be responsible, and being on a team removes the need for the individual to provide all the motivation. When the team's purpose is clear, and on good teams it always is; when the individual members have a voice in making the standards; when there are strong relationships between the teammates; when skills are shared and utilized; when everyone has a role on the team—then responsibility isn't hard at all.

COMMITMENT
Is devoted to a shared vision and a greater purpose. Sets high expectations and fully commits to one's role, to the process, and to the team. Is dedicated to reaching goals and helping others achieve.

Commitment is a loaded word, the kind of word that onscreen coaches scream at their players in impassioned halftime speeches. But what does it mean to be committed to a team, really? Over time, commitment level can get stronger or it can diminish. Even the most fanatical of team members has a personal life filled with hardships, setbacks, disappointments, heartbreak, and loss that can impact their commitment to a team.

Every team usually has at least one person who is fully committed at any given time; some teams have several. But, like all mental talent, commitment can be developed. The goal is to achieve a team full of committed people who are on a common mission together; these teams are virtually unstoppable. This process can be broken down into three areas.

Vision and purpose

The first part of the process involves the collective creation of a vision and purpose. People always want to be part of something bigger than themselves, something special, something remarkable. This is why most people join a team. Establish a collective purpose that is grand, far reaching, and inclusive of everyone. This is not about short-term goals but about the legacy and impact the team hopes to have on each other, on the community, and on humanity. This gives team members a reason to be present, to be hopeful.

Goals

The second part of inspiring commitment involves team and personal goals. Both are important. Goals shouldn't be pie in the sky impossibilities; they have to be concrete and attainable. Teams and individuals have a much better chance of achieving their goals when they are cultivated by everyone as opposed to being mandated from the top. Goals can change, but the team's practice of goal-setting and continually working towards specific goals can not.

Keep in mind that the good of the team has to come first. Are some people only pursuing personal goals and disguising them as team goals or are they really understanding their teammates' goals and formulating plans to help them get there? Going back to trust and relationships, does everyone on the team know the dreams and passions of their teammates? Do you understand their fears, their strengths, their weaknesses? This is the starting point for developing stronger commitment in everyone. Focus on developing team goals together while sharing personal goals with each other.

The best players should know the personal goals and dreams of the guys on the bench. And the guys on the bench should know the personal goals and dreams of the best athletes. In business, the top executives and managers should know the goals and dreams of the employees so their talents can be cultivated and everyone can share in their success when goals are met.

When people start to commit to helping their teammates achieve their personal goals, the team becomes unstoppable. It's yet another form of magic, of chemistry; teams that bond and help each other in other areas of their lives become stronger, more likely to succeed at work or on the field.

A role for everyone

The third part of fostering commitment on your team involves establishing meaningful roles for everyone. Everyone has a unique talent to bring to the table; there is a place for every member of a team. Roles may never appear equal, but they do have equal value in the ultimate success of the team. A big part of any team member's success is their capacity to not only accept their role, but to excel in it. Roles can change, and they can change often. Great teams are always prepared for these changes.

Every team member may not be one hundred percent committed now, and that is okay. Commitment evolves as team members find their place on the team, take ownership, and find ways to help their teammates. And don't be offended when some players are not initially as committed as others. Find a way to help get them there by exposing their true talents, by understanding their personal dreams, and by creating an impactful vision and greater purpose.

Bill Russell said, "Commitment separates those who live their dreams from those that live their lives regretting the opportunities they have squandered."

PASSION
Pursues legacy with positive energy, optimism, and a fierce desire to be great at what is loved. Builds team pride and cares about team success. Supports the dreams and passions of teammates.

Former Indiana University head basketball coach Tom Crean, said it best: "If you're not bringing energy to your teammates or coaching staff, then you are taking it from them. Surround yourself with people who bring you energy and ones that look forward to yours." Passion drives the energy that fuels the greatest teams. For many team members who are talented, who love their work or their sport, passion might seem like second nature. Here's the wrinkle: passion is a skill that must be shared.

Most people want others to be successful. Most people want to be useful, helpful. But the world is also full of disruptors, anarchists, and selfish people. The disruptor enjoys chaos and pandemonium; disruptors will cause havoc as a goal. Disruptors exist in a lawless and wild state; they interfere with unity, often without even meaning to. And the selfish? We need only look in the mirror; we are all selfish in some aspect of our lives. The key is not to let our more selfish impulses run the show.

So the extreme teammate has multiple responsibilities. One, they have to know their own passions and pursue them. Two, they have to know their teammates and what their passions are; this requires time and honesty and trust. Three, they have to work hard at helping their teammates cultivate their passions. Sometimes they have to be a counselor. Sometimes they have to pry, dig, push, prod. Sometimes extreme teammates have to help team members discover their dreams, and when they do, everyone involved will be overwhelmed with a sense of accomplishment.

Passion is the foundation for a team's motivation, enthusiasm, and optimism. Passion is about the pursuit of legacy; it's about chasing the thing that you love. It's about creating a strong sense of pride within the team. Team pride is created when people know each other well, understand and pursue their passions and dreams together, and work as a united force.

Passion is about working hard, staying open, being honest, weathering the bad times, and working towards the good.

COMMUNICATION
Speaks with truth and dignity. Uses positive words, shows good body language, listens to understand and doesn't let people complain or criticize. Demands transparency and respect in communication.

The way people communicate can make or break a team. Communication is a driver of your team's culture, and it isn't just about the words you are using. Communication includes actions, body language, and what *isn't* said.

Communication is always a reflection of culture. In a team with a strong culture, communication includes clear expectations, transparency, honesty, equal voice, respect for opinions, dignity, good body language, positive word usage, and knowing how to listen to understand.

Coach Mike Krzyzewski says that "effective teamwork begins and ends with communication." Body language, hand gestures, actions— everything is communication, whether you know it or not. Extreme teammates know how to communicate everything with pure honesty and for the benefit of everyone, not just for themselves. If a teammate is upset about something, an extreme teammate makes sure the person is heard and might suggest they communicate to the coach or leader. They don't allow communication that can be destructive to the culture. They don't allow people to be critical or complain. They listen intently but know when and where to draw the line based on how the communication is affecting team culture. Successful teams are always talking when they are competing—this comes naturally when there is established trust within the group. The communication has to be positive, founded on trust and focused on winning, on improvement. Naysaying, doom and gloom, the insurmountable—these belong in the garbage can.

A team's communication must be focused on the desired outcome. I had a teammate once who, despite being fast and skilled, gave up when a game started to turn against him. He would loaf, pretend not to care. It was a defense mechanism that hurt everyone else. I confronted him once, but it didn't end well. I had failed to first establish a strong trust, so my comments offended him, were perceived as critical instead of helpful. My intentions were good, but my teammate did not notice; he couldn't see the big picture because I never painted it for him.

Questions to ask yourself as you guide your team to excellent communication: who is leading in this area? Is everyone involved? Does everyone share the same expectations regarding communication? Are there systems, standards, and structures in place that promote transparent communication?

Remember: the primary way we experience reality is through *language*. The words we use matter. Words reflect thoughts. Thoughts dictate action. Communication is nothing less than the way we see ourselves, the way we see the world, and the way we decide to carry ourselves through that world.

Communicating isn't just talking, it's also listening. And listening is not the same thing as hearing. When people are truly listening, they have to work to understand. This is crucial to building trust and loyalty. If you don't understand something someone has said, ask them to explain it. Pay attention. If people don't listen to each other, they'll never *understand* each other and will miss out on each other's life stories. And without understanding, they'll never be able to help each other pursue their dreams, the things that really matter.

There is no in-between; team communication is either strong or weak. It is all determined by what is allowed and what is not allowed within the group.

Currently, what do people do if something is bothering them on the team? Do team members tend to keep their grievances to themselves, or perhaps only tell certain friends, creating a dangerous divide in the team, or do they take the more difficult route and communicate openly when necessary? Is there a system in place for voicing concerns? If not, there should be.

Like the other elements of building a great culture, communication can be nurtured and taught. And every team has capable, transparent, and honest communicators that can help inspire mastery in the entire team. If that is you, step up.

For those of us who have not already achieved communication mastery, there is hope. We have to value relationships and create strong trust. Once we have created that trust, we must have the courage to share opinions, issues, and problems in a respectful way. Nobody is a mind-reader. We must be honest and speak the truth because everyone deserves honest, constructive feedback. Dallas Cowboys coach Tom Landry said: "There's a misconception about teamwork. Teamwork is the ability to have different thoughts about things; it's the ability to argue and stand up and say loud and strong what you feel. But in the end, it's also the ability to adjust to what is best for the team." Speak the truth, but also be ready to listen and to adapt.

To anyone paying attention, body language says everything a person is thinking. Watch the body language of world-class athletes. They panther around when they walk, often on the balls of the feet. Their shoulders are straight, and they face the world with open hearts and clear eyes. They aren't sulking or sluggish; they move with purpose and power. They make walking, even standing still, look like a statement.

Someone with poor body language might be able to hide their thoughts for a little while, but eventually the frustration of keeping their true feelings hidden will deplete their energy and, in a way that is almost supernatural, deplete the energy of the people around them.

Poor body language is both childish and selfish. It destroys enthusiasm, teamwork, and togetherness. On your team, reinforce the idea that everyone must present themselves with dignity and respect. Walk and talk with pride in yourself and expect it from the team. Body language can be one of the hardest things to change in an athlete.

Words also matter, and they matter a lot. Jimmy Johnson, former coach of the Dallas Cowboys, was always aware of the words he used. He never said "don't fumble the ball." Instead, he would say "take care of the ball." Follow his example. Phrase things in the positive. This should be an expectation of everyone, not just the coach.

Everyone on the team, including the coaching staff and its leaders, should make an effort to stop using the word "I" and replace it with "we," otherwise, declarations that should be uniting—"We're going to win state"—turn arrogant and self-serving—"I want to win state." You'd be surprised how effective it is when everyone puts the team's business in the plural. "We played a tough game" instead of "I played a tough game." It removes the singular captain or leader and puts everyone in the same boat together. This simple switch solidifies the culture.

Communication is also about addressing mistakes and helping other players get over obstacles. Everyone has an obligation to offer constructive feedback, but teammates don't have the right to be critical of each other. Extreme teammates know the difference and only tolerate truthful communication that is shared with dignity and in a spirit of selflessness and genuine compassion and concern for others. Complainers keep complaining when they know people will listen. Gradually complainers attract other complainers; extreme teammates never let this happen. Complainers usually lack courage, so standing up to them is really not that hard, but it must be done if you want to defend the culture and be on a team of forward-looking, optimistic achievers.

There's an NBA player who would, he admits, chirp critical things at certain players from the bench so the coach would hear. He wanted more playing time and thought that bad-mouthing his own teammates would persuade the coach to make substitutions. Essentially, it was his way of getting back in the game quicker. He clearly had God-given talent and a strong work ethic—he made it into the NBA, after all—but he was a terrible teammate. He put himself in front of his team and, in shameless self-promotion, ran down the very people he should have been building up. He will never sniff the hall of fame even though he had the physical talent to get there. Instead, he's just another person who will one day look back and see how much of his talent he wasted by being selfish.

Secrets, personal agendas, gossip—these are poison to a team's culture. Everyone has to work to be transparent and open, and everyone has to work to bring this out in each other. Silence is just as damaging as joining in a chorus of complaint. When a team member criticizes or blames a teammate, others have to step in to stop this type of destructive communication—a loser mentality. Extreme teammates have the courage to be bold and brave; they get in the way if necessary.

There's a final component to communication: how we communicate with ourselves. You have to condition yourself to ask the right questions so your brain hears the right answers. This is a form of grace that you need to extend to yourself. If you condition yourself to ask destructive questions, you will get destructive answers. For instance, if you ask yourself "why didn't coach play me in the second half?" or "why have I been passed up for this promotion?" your brain will provide countless negative answers that will tear down your confidence, many of which won't be true. But if you condition your brain to ask positive questions, for example: "What do I need to do to play in the second half?" or "What do I need to do to get that promotion?" you will get answers that you can use. As a result, you will work harder, compete harder, do what it takes. This approach builds character.

Once you operate in this manner, you will be able to protect the team culture and encourage this kind of internal communication from your teammates when they might be struggling. This is being an extreme teammate.

ACCOUNTABILITY
Takes ownership of the team by enforcing team standards. Holds people accountable, leads by example, reinforces team expectations, and excels in assigned role. Demands accountability from others.

The driving force of a culture is the team's standards and expectations. Team standards or rules should be set by the entire team, where everyone has a voice, otherwise they are just a leader's rules and mandates. If the standards are set by the team, then everyone will feel responsible for enforcing them. Collective standards means collective ownership. And no one wants to break their own rules.

Accountability can be a scary word. It often summons up notions of punishment and consequences. In school, we're often conditioned to see accountability as something heavy, a weight that's there to crush people when they make a mistake.

Of course, this isn't what accountability is at all. Hand in hand with responsibility and commitment, true accountability first and foremost is utilized by the individuals on a team; each teammate works to meet the team's standards. Extreme teammates will hold each other accountable for the good of the team, not to the detriment of individuals. Accountability is a tool. A gauge that lets team members know how effective they are. Don't be afraid of it. Embrace it. Team standards create opportunities. Don't run away from them.

Sometimes this is tricky. For instance, allowing something to happen that breaks the team standards can be worse than the actual transgression itself. Here we have the notion of consent: anything you don't confront, you are agreeing to. So a kind of moral erosion can take place when people don't enforce the standards. As a coach, I've often seen teams on this slippery slope. For example, after prodding by a coach, a player might continue to do something wrong on defense, usually it can be more powerful when a teammate steps up and deals with this relatively minor infraction.

A team's culture is only as strong as its standards. And the standards are only as strong as the players who enforce them. Never lower those standards to appease anyone. If someone is holding you to high standards, be thankful and consider yourself fortunate. Sometimes you will need to be the one holding your teammates accountable; accept responsibility and correct teammates when they need correction. Enforcing standards might seem difficult at first, but view it as a gift. By holding your teammates accountable, you are looking out for their best interests.

As former NBA player and coach Scott Skiles said, "You know you have something really special when the players start holding themselves accountable." When every person, regardless of their talent, enforces standards—because there is a shared commitment and shared purpose—great things happen. This is the magic of teamwork. Collective empowerment creates success.

WORK ETHIC
Improves skills with efficient, intelligent, and uncomfortable hard work. Gets better every day and creates good habits from repetition, attention to detail, and discipline. Pushes others and builds work ethic.

Your work ethic carries over to every aspect of your life. The reaching and striving, the never giving up, the always going for first, the competitive fire, the detail-oriented discipline is all part of a team's work ethic. When former great players look back on their careers, they typically recall the work as hard but also fun. And they always show gratitude to the people that pushed them to work so hard. "Far and away the best prize that life offers," Teddy Roosevelt said, "is the chance to work hard at work worth doing."

Teams can build their capacity for work ethic. This happens when hard-working team members demand the same work ethic from the rest of the team. If you're that person, start demanding.

Look: discipline is mandatory, details are mandatory, and being uncomfortable is mandatory if you want to connect your goals to accomplishment. People cannot achieve anything, in any area, without sweat and sacrifice, hard work and determination. Your habits are creating you. Details matter. When people are competing at a high level, every inch matters, every second matters. Runners beat each other by milliseconds, high jumpers by fractions of inches. The difference is often all the work viewers and fans never see.

One of the best teams I ever coached had a fierce and wild passion for details and working hard, and everyone tried to win every little drill. No one gave an inch and no one asked for one. We conditioned ourselves to fight for everything, and it translated into victory in games.

We became a team of extreme teammates. The players influenced each other with their work ethic, their passion, their discipline, and their attention to detail. They motivated each other. They all pitched in and did extra work. One player led some of the leaner teammates in off-season workouts he designed himself. No one wanted to play us. We knew we could beat anybody.

Work ethic builds confidence and creates competitiveness, perseverance, and all the rest of the intangibles we need to be successful in sports, in business, and in life. People with a mediocre work ethic get mediocre results. Nobody should ever be able to question your team's work ethic. Your team might not be the strongest, the fastest, or the most skilled, but they can always be the hardest working.

NBA great Steve Nash once said: "If everyone worked as hard as me I would be out of a job." It's great when one person can work extremely hard, but when that one person can influence an entire team through work ethic, remarkable things happen.

MOTIVATION
Is self-driven, ambitious, and an inspiration for hope. Uses unfairness, oversights, and failure as motivation. Chases excellence with determination and patience. Over-prepares so the team overachieves.

Let's get it out of the way up front: Life can be unfair. Absorb this lesson now and then get over it. There is no reward for the most thoroughly defeated.

Everything must be earned and everyone has opportunities. Some more than others, for sure, but everyone has some. Don't cast yourself as a victim. Don't allow victimhood to enter the team's mindset. Instead, use the obstacles in your way as motivation. Create your own path to greatness. I'll say it again: Protect the team from making excuses. That way lies failure.

It's a lesson as old as time: Never give up. The greats keep battling, always. Watch your favorite athletes in a game where their team is losing. The motivated players don't slump their shoulders; they don't shuffle around; they go out there and try to take control of the game. They fight through it. The greats are relentless. The greats are ruthless.

They are also patient. Motivated people understand that it takes time to improve; it takes even longer to reach perfection. But the motivation never dissipates.

Motivation is connected to work ethic and accountability; it shows itself in how teams prepare. Kobe Bryant, a teen phenom and worldwide sensation just out of high school, worked harder than most people, in practice and in games. He was amazingly motivated. Motivated people know how to prepare; they prepare both physically and mentally and they demand the same from others. Passion creates motivation, and motivation is the driving force that separates the good from the great. Motivated people have an unmatched work ethic; they become legendary through preparation. Passion plus motivation plus work ethic equals confidence and success.

I've never seen a team over-prepare. I *have* seen a weaker team, through hard work and focus, beat a stronger team. It happens all the time. Being fully and completely prepared as a team is in itself a great feeling; it allows teams to compete to their fullest, with collective confidence, fueled by a mission and ready to achieve things that nobody else believed they could.

Bill Parcels said it best: "The game is won or lost before the game is played."

CHAPTER 6
Climate that Overachieves

Achieving greatness, becoming a team that wins championships, a team that people remember—takes hundreds of different puzzle pieces falling into place. Some pieces appear less important than others, but they are all essential for the final result. The reliable rebounder is just as important as the star shooter. The bench player, the pinch runner, the eleventh man, the walk-on who works hard in practice, even the equipment manager who prepares the equipment for each game. Everyone has a role to play and they should all be valued equally.

Every great team since the dawn of time has shared one crucial quality. They work harder as a team than they do as individuals. They reach beyond their abilities. In a word, they overachieve.

Overachievers are people who accomplish more than anyone considered possible. Overachievers perform regardless of God-given talent; they transcend the limits of their physical abilities by leveraging their mental abilities. Overachievers want to win. They fight. They scrap. They go the extra mile.

Once your team has the foundation, once your culture is solid and your team is performing in areas of effort, execution, competitiveness, enthusiasm, and perseverance; when your team members are focused and selfless, working to help each other;

when the team has standards in place that everyone buys into and everyone enforces, then overachievement is inevitable.

If you ask any experienced coach to reminisce about some of their greatest teams, the ones that brought them the most pride, inevitably they will talk about the ones that overachieved.

Overachievement does not require enormous reserves of raw talent. Instead, it relies on team dynamics, team culture, selfless teammates, and wild enthusiasm. Because great teammates and great teams are made, not born. Competing above your head, surprising yourself with your accomplishments, mastering techniques through preparation and then using that technique in new and exciting ways—these are some of the ways overachievement manifests.

Talk to any hall of famer in any sport and the first thing they'll bring up—after all the accolades, after all the publicity, after all the money—is what their teammates thought of them, what they did for each other, and how they overachieved professionally because of the people around them. These same people usually go on to apply the same framework of overachievement, outlined below, to the business world.

APPLICATION
Is coachable, curious, and reflective. Listens, observes, applies instruction, and uses feedback. Takes risks and learns from mistakes. Asks questions and accelerates growth by teaching others.

Bill Parcels says that "you can easily separate 'team guys' from the 'me guys' by how they accept coaching. The guys that accept it are about winning." Overachieving people never resist coaching.

Fear can suppress our growth, but when the entire team is completely involved and responsible for learning, fears go out the window. Some people are visual learners, some people learn by doing, some people need demonstrations, some need handouts, and some need a lot of repetition. Some people can read a manual and get it. Others need to perform. Make sure everyone on your team has the opportunity to be coached, instructed, or taught in a way that makes sense to them. When everyone takes ownership to ensure that everyone learns, then your progress as a team will be monumental, and the process can actually be quite fun.

Start by always knowing the *why* behind what you and your teammates are learning. Knowing this will give everyone the creative ability and confidence to teach the new skill, concept, or strategy to others.

Look. Someone on your team is already great at teaching. Inspire these people to come forward so they can take ownership of this area. They can assist with teaching, but, more importantly, they can assist with creating a team full of learners, teachers, and mentors. Remember, application and teaching are mental talents and everyone has the potential to improve a mental talent. Greatness is just around the corner when each person goes out of their way to help coach or teach their teammates. Teaching is one of the best ways to learn. Teaching actually makes people more coachable and unleashes their ability to comprehend.

What are people doing in the back of the line? Are they wondering about the next drill or are they watching teammates to help with technique? At work are people checking out when they have down time later or are they thinking of ways to train their coworkers to be more efficient? Are people just standing around expecting someone else to do all the teaching or is everyone watching to make sure team members get it right? Are people contributing by sharing what they learned, or are they holding back their expertise because they're afraid someone might take their job?

It's your teammates, in particular, that will provide the most impactful feedback of your career. Listen to each other. Ask questions. Crave feedback and seek it out.

FOCUS

Visualizes perfection and success. Uses a clear mindset to concentrate, relax, and focus on achieving specific tasks. Avoids distractions and keeps everyone focused on roles, goals, and mission.

It's a universal truth in sports: you don't hit home runs by focusing on hitting home runs. You don't win championships by focusing on the final game. No. You focus on the small things first. You hit home runs by focusing on the ball. You win championships by focusing on each game, chopped into manageable lengths of time. One play at a time, minute by minute, quarter by quarter.

Focus. It's a skill and power of the mind that everyone on a team can cultivate and develop if they work together. It's an essential skill and the very lifeblood of competition. As Celtics great Bill Russel said: "Concentration and mental toughness are the margins of victory." Complete focus allows you to relax other parts of your brain and body. Complete focus from everyone enables teams to overachieve when everything is on the line. Many extremely successful business people, including Bill Gates and Warren Buffet, have credited focus as the single most important factor in their success.

You can see which athletes are focused before a game. They exude a calm seriousness and take in the world with stern eyes. They perform their pre-game rituals with a serene intensity. You can see which teams are focused during pre-game. They never glance over at the upcoming opponent; they are too focused on what they need to do and what they can control. Everyone gets pre-game jitters now and then, but when teams are focused as a result of preparation, nerves disappear because they are thinking about each other instead of themselves. Focused teams don't have big peaks and valleys in big games; they execute their talents throughout, giving their best.

Great team focus comes from team members' dogged determination to execute their roles with perfection and their commitment to keeping each other's attention on the task at hand through uncomfortable situations in practice that stretch and challenge the ability to stay focused. This is part of your team's mental training, how you craft your own mind and thoughts. Whatever you allow the team to focus on is what you will get. If the team is focused on how cold it is, the team will be cold. If the team is focused on how tough the opponent is, the team will become timid. If the team is focused on how bad the officiating is, the team will rely on excuses to explain their failures.

Focus comes from a commitment to doing only what is in front of you, an ability to ignore the big things and visualize yourself accomplishing the small things. It's the small things within everyone's specified role that matter most.

Everyone has the ability to develop great focus. If the stakes are high enough in your mind, everyone will be able to stay attentive to the task at hand. Focus is one of the easiest skills to influence in your teammates. If you mean business, others will join you.

Don't allow distractions to get in the way of your team's focus. It takes *focus* to focus, and if that sounds silly or strange, well, show me a great athlete who is texting on the sidelines during timeouts. Show me a great athlete who is looking for someone in the crowd during a big game. You can't because great athletes do not allow distractions to get in the way. Your team shouldn't, either. Extreme teammates keep each other focused.

Like every basketball coach, I've asked teams to stand on the baseline and watch players attempt free throws. Their eyes often glaze over; they start moving around; they can barely watch. Then, when I say that for each missed free throw the whole team runs a suicide, their attention snaps further into place. And when I pull out a hundred-dollar bill and ask a player to shoot for money, everything changes. Their body language changes, their form changes, everything becomes more significant. The teammates on the baseline become more interested. Now, the point of this exercise isn't to highlight the importance of money. No, the point is simple: everyone has the potential to modify their focus. It's a decision, but sometimes we need a nudge from our teammates to make sure we're making the right decision.

PERSEVERANCE
Never gives up. Embraces and faces adversity and uses setbacks as opportunities to get stronger. Competes with a forward-thinking attitude and challenges teammates to overcome difficulties.

Winston Churchill's final message as prime minister of England was a single sentence: "Never, ever, ever give up." Churchill thrived in the most difficult time in England's history. In the midst of the grim challenges facing his nation and the world, he embraced adversity. He found the very meaning of his life in it.

What Churchill had, in spades, was perseverance. This is the persistence and resolution to accomplish something despite obstacles and delays. Perseverance is related to attitude and work ethic. Just like focus, teams can build perseverance.

A few things to keep in mind. One, whatever challenges your team faces will prepare you for the future. In sports, business, and life, history always repeats itself. Two, embrace adversity. We are creatures that evolved through adaptation; the very essence of being human is struggle. Three, recast your challenges as opportunities and possibilities. Playing the best team in the league? You have the opportunity to compete against the best. Lost a star player to an injury? Someone else has the chance to step up and make a difference. No one accomplishes anything without struggle, obstacles, setbacks, and even failures. "Show me someone who has done something worthwhile," Lou Holtz said, "and I'll show you someone who has overcome adversity."

Don't misunderstand. Adversity hurts; losing hurts, but experiencing the pain of losing and of failure is *good*. Don't insulate the team from loss or from disappointment.

In fact, failure and pain are superb motivators. They force a team to grow. So view a difficult situation as a gift. Extreme teammates embrace these gifts, know things will get better, and don't let anyone quit.

Condition the team to think forward, not backward. Focus on the next play, the next game, the next opportunity with a determined sense of optimism. Tough times go away when tough-minded people persevere. Negative reflection during competition will never produce a positive result.

Don Flowers was a former college football coach who coached at East Richland High School in Olney, Illinois. I was part of his staff in my very first job as a teacher and assistant football coach. We were both hired at the same time, but he was the experienced coach taking over a football program that needed to be revived. I was a young coach with energy and enthusiasm but little experience.

We had some talent on our team, but it takes time for players to learn a new system. After we started the season 0-3, the entire coaching staff was sitting around in our tiny cramped office after a miserable game. The atmosphere was gloomy; we were facing a season of straight losses.

Then a player knocked at the door. He was a crafty, solid linebacker, and he looked perplexed and lost as he entered the room. "Coach, this just isn't working," he said. "I think I want to quit."

Coach Flowers looked at him without any hesitation and said, "Look around! We all want to quit right now, you think you're the only one? You think you're the only player that wants to give up?" The player looked confused. This wasn't what he was expecting. Flowers continued, "You know what? I want to quit, too. But I won't." He sized the linebacker up. "You can do what you want, but think about it first. Come talk to me in the morning. But realize something. Once you quit, quitting will be easy. It will be easy to quit a job, easy to quit a marriage, easy to quit a lot of things in your life." Coach Flowers cracked this off without anger and then turned his attention away from the linebacker, who left without another word. I wasn't sure what to say, but the linebacker showed up to our next practice.

Fast forward six weeks. We gathered in the end zone after winning the last game of the regular season to reach the playoffs with a record of 5-4. In the dark, cool air of a fast-approaching winter, that same kid stood up in front of everyone with a hint of tears in eyes and said, "Coach, thanks for not letting me quit."

Coach Flowers was right. Quitting isn't a small thing or a momentary defeat. Quitting is about walking away from any kind of struggle. It's about accepting failure into your heart. Worse, if you quit on a team in the middle of a season, you will carry this knowledge with you for *the rest of your life*. It's one thing to outgrow a sport or move your life in a different direction, but you have to stay true to your commitments. Otherwise you'll carry around regret and make excuses forever.

The immortal Babe Ruth said, "It's hard to beat a person that never gives up."

CONFIDENCE
Has unshakable confidence from total preparation. Makes teammates better and plays with poise and composure. Strongly believes in oneself and makes other people believe in themselves.

Confidence comes from trust, preparation, and a strong work ethic. Like many of the other mental talents mentioned in this book, teams can build confidence. And when your team builds confidence together, you will be much more competitive. Confidence will bring composure and poise. False confidence is borne out of arrogance; real confidence comes from attention to detail, discipline, and hours of sweat equity. Real confidence is a hard-earned skill. Real confidence instills belief—in yourself, in your team, and in the team's goals and vision.

Lack of confidence is the bane of an athlete's sports life. I've seen very talented players begin to falter. They overthink. They second-guess. They lose faith in their basic abilities. I've seen world-beaters get out-rebounded and out-run because their confidence was gone. I've seen superb athletes dither and wither. It's a terrible sight. It happens when teammates let it happen.

So, two things: one, everyone's confidence slips sometimes. And two, you and your teammates are obligated to help each other when this happens.

Put another way: the people who reach the pinnacle of self-confidence must influence self-confidence in their teammates. Believing in yourself means you are prepared to make your teammates believe in themselves. Believing in yourself is crucial; self-doubt—and this is a plague on every player's thoughts from time to time—is a killer. But you must move from self-confidence to team confidence. Teammates should help each other believe not only in themselves but also in one another. Achieving this is an enormous competitive advantage.

You cannot fake belief in each other. In tough competitions, the masks are dropped. You have to invest in one another, as we've said throughout this book, in a variety of ways. In terms of building up confidence, you cannot offer generic clichés. You must have a relationship with your teammates to be able to even speak to their strengths. It doesn't cost anything to give compliments and power statements to teammates, but it often pays back tenfold. Remember, self-confidence is a crucial first step, but the goal is team confidence.

Some people are reluctant to build up their teammates because they fear being surpassed or overlooked if someone else is getting ahead. Obviously, this is selfish thinking. The extreme teammate builds up every member of the team. They give compliments when they can, constructive criticism when they must. Extreme teammates are engaging in nothing less than the holy work of improving other people's lives. "There is no greater compliment for a player," Don Meyer said, "than to be told that he makes his teammates better."

In 2008, the New York Giants were playing in the NFL championship game against the Green Bay Packers at Lambeau Field. The game was tied in overtime. Fourth down on the 29-yard line, and Giants head coach Tom Coughlin had to decide whether to punt or go for the field goal. Lawrence Tynes had already missed two field goals—one from the 43-yard line, one from the 36-yard line—that could've won the game and a trip to the Super Bowl.

Coughlin was looking around for his kicker when he realized that Tynes was already on the field. "I looked right at him, and when I saw him out there, it made a very strong impression," Coughlin said. "I knew he was feeling very confident. I was looking for a sign, and that was it."

A lot of players would have been rattled by the prospect of another attempt—this one an even longer kick—after two misses. But Tynes wasn't. He nailed the field goal and the Giants went on to the Super Bowl, where they beat Tom Brady and the New England Patriots in a massive upset.

Despite the misses, Tynes knew he was prepared, mentally and physically. He didn't let his confidence get shaken. He believed in himself. His belief was contagious. And his team was victorious.

ENTHUSIASM

Uses a positive attitude to solve problems, encourage teammates, and keep things fun. Brings out the best in people, spreads positivity, and inspires the team with a contagious spirit.

It's what we strive for but it's nearly impossible to stay positive all the time, in sports, at work, or in our home lives. There are too many variables, a million things that can go wrong no matter how confident, prepared, passionate, or committed you are—even great teams doing everything right will lose sometimes.

But it's not impossible to stay enthusiastic. It's not impossible to stay hungry. With enthusiasm, the team will weather the storms, they will beat the odds, they will achieve the insurmountable.

Enthusiasm isn't for empty show; enthusiasm drowns out negative thoughts. It inspires other people. It cultivates belief and a can-do attitude. Enthusiasm keeps the team focused on their goals and their purpose. Enthusiasm revels in fun, creates opportunities and an attitude of possibility. Finally, enthusiasm is a conduit for delight and joy. You won't overthink or second-guess when your team is in the zone of pure joy.

So, yes, sometimes positivity will lag. But the team can stay enthusiastic and optimistic, even about the little things. Average teammates will let the moment dictate the energy they bring. But extreme teammates use enthusiasm in every moment to create the energy the team needs to be successful. Enthusiasm belongs at the center of any important work in life, but is often overlooked when a team is caught up in preparation and hard work. Don't let enthusiasm slide to the background; it will keep team members invested and focused, and their enthusiasm will radiate off each other, inspiring greatness in an infinite positive feedback loop.

Rick Loeffelholz is the head coach of the boy's swim team at Dubuque Hempstead High School and the president of the Iowa High School Swim Coaches Association. I was fortunate enough to conduct a seminar for his swim team, and Rick shared a story with me about an amazing swimmer named David.

On top of being a great athlete, David was constantly building others up and encouraging them to do their best. One of the team's traditions is to have the guys give an award to a swimmer of the meet for each dual meet throughout the season. When David was a junior, he found a hub cap after a team breakfast. He brought it to practice and asked if anyone had lost it. No one claimed it, so he asked if they could use it as the award. He spray-painted it gold and hung it on a chain so the winner could lead the team out wearing the hub cap at meets. It was goofy, but it was also an important ritual that helped the team stay enthusiastic—a reminder to have fun.

Rituals are a great way to build and maintain enthusiasm. Be creative, think outside the box, and do things that inspire others.

Anyone can bring enthusiasm, but every team has people that can excel in this role if we open the door for each other. This role has extreme value; it can change the trajectory of a team.

Create a climate where spirit is contagious.

CHAPTER 7
Highly Competitive Environment

In addition to all of the qualities discussed above, there are six pillars that are essential to achieving excellence in highly competitive environments: intelligence, role execution, competitiveness, toughness, effort, and selflessness. These items are the culmination of proper preparation, strong culture, and a thriving climate. They are the final ingredients in the team masterpiece, the non-negotiable characteristics that bring greatness.

INTELLIGENCE
Makes good decisions and manages time wisely. Knows time and score, studies the competition and adjusts the strategy to gain advantages. Utilizes everyone's creativity, innovation, and intelligence.

Nobody is smarter than the insights, creativity, and innovation of the collective group. By blending the intelligence of every team member, teams will find solutions they never thought possible; they will have ideas that are different but necessary; they will get buy-in from the group because everyone's intelligence is being put to work. Some people are intelligent at simplifying problems, some people are great at strategy, some people can make great predictions about their opponents. All intelligence has value. And everyone has something to offer.

Intelligence in sports is rarely mentioned. Like other mental talents, it is often subsumed by a physical performance. We often overstate the importance of individual talent and underestimate the importance of team's collective intelligence. This is how great teams and great businesses separate themselves from the competition.

Part of your intelligence is your decision-making as a team—did you make the smartest move? Did you try to do something beyond your abilities? Did you recover in the smartest and fastest possible way? Did you trick your opponent into playing your game? Did you control the pace? There's a saying from ancient history: as above, so below. How you practice is how you will play. And, in a sense, how you live is how you will practice. So good decision-making should be marbled into every facet of your life.

Time management is a collective skill that is routinely overlooked, and it is one that requires intelligence. Extreme teammates don't necessarily work fifteen hours a day, but they do manage their time intelligently. Practice is sacred. Focus on how everyone can be maximally effective in the allotted time. This requires being wise, judicious, and determined. Can teammates talk more during practice? Can teammates teach more? Can teammates share more of their knowledge?

A sure sign of intelligence is being able to consider other options, other points of view. There are great benefits to being open-minded, open to new ideas. Intelligent people are not wedded to a single technique or method. Strategies evolve, often from unlikely sources, from the kid at the end of the bench or the intern schlepping the coffees. Be open to everyone's intelligence. Innovation comes from applied creativity and the collective knowledge of a group. Find the value in other people's ideas and don't be scared to share your own. An idea might seem foolish on the surface, but when added to another idea, you might have unlocked a problem, overcome an obstacle, advanced to a new level.

The key point: the collective and collaborative intelligence of your team is a potent and formidable tool, and it needs to be applied.

As in sports, so in business. Recently I had a conversation with a business leadership consultant. His job was training executives for Fortune 500 companies. I asked him what he thought was the biggest challenge to overcome when trying to convince top executives to change their leadership style. His answer: "Humility."

He went on to explain that "many top executives in well-established companies got there by doing it their own way and don't see the need to change. Many believe in the top-down approach. And some," he continued, "get close to retirement and it isn't worth their time."

"So how do you get anyone to change?" I asked, genuinely curious.

He wasn't optimistic. "Some people change," he said, "but many don't. Once they've experienced some success using one formula they think it's the only way. What they don't see is that the competition is gaining on them and will be in a strong position to overtake them."

Your collective intelligence is one of your greatest mental gifts, and so many people take it for granted. Stay hungry. Stay awake and curious. Never stop learning and never stop thinking.

ROLE EXECUTION
Achieves synergy when all roles are executed together with perfection. Pushes the group to execute each role with continuity and perform with consistency. Becomes an unstoppable machine.

Execution happens when every single person thrives in their expected role. Nature gives us plenty of examples of this. Deer are like cats; they often do their own thing. They are fleet creatures, fast and tough. But a pack of wolves, they work together to make a kill. The faster, older, slower, and younger wolves all have different roles. Those roles can eventually change, but they always work together to find strength for the greater good. Which would you bet on, a single deer or a pack of wolves? When the wolves are all working together, they achieve the synergy of a great team, where the whole is greater than the sum of its parts. Great teams achieve synergy. Mediocre teams never come close.

Synergy begins with trust, which builds to commitment and accountability. Synergy is derived from superior focus and relies on selflessness. And most important—without execution, there is no synergy. The teams that achieve synergy peak at the right time, they come together, they figure it out, and each team member excels at their given role.

The main killer of synergy—which is a fancy way of saying continuity and chemistry—is a person's ego. Think of the wolves. They aren't worried about style, or who is going to nab their dinner; they are stalking their prey. They are engaged in the essence of their work. They are executing their roles above all else.

Every role has great value to the team. In *The Art of War*, Sun Tzu says: "Victory does not rely upon numbers but upon the united hearts of those that fight." It's everyone's job to accept and excel in their role so that hearts become united for the good of the team.

If there are people on the team who are not sure about their role, help and encourage clarity as soon as possible. If there are team members who aren't excited about their roles, help them see the value in their job, help them find the spark, the fun, the passion they can bring to their corner of the team, however seemingly unglamorous or unsung. And, if you're not happy with your current role, dig in, work harder, move up, but remember: in the words of theater great Konstantin Stanislavski: "There are no small parts, only small actors."

When the individual members accept their roles, when timing becomes precise, and when team execution becomes more important than personal execution, you become a consistent and unstoppable machine.

COMPETITIVENESS
Finds a way to win. Uses inner strength, will power, and a competitive drive to rise to the occasion and conquer team expectations. Gets people to compete at their highest level.

In a 1988 game, Michael Jordan scored fifty-nine points against the Detroit Pistons, a remarkable display of basketball prowess. This was before the streak of championship titles, and many people, especially in the media, were still labeling Jordan a selfish player who would never win a championship, comparing him to Dominique Wilkins.

Boy, were they wrong.

Directly after that game back in 1988, sportscaster Pat O'Brien asked Jordan a couple of questions. "You're acting like you just won the world championship, big game for you?"

Jordan replied, "It was. We played a very exceptional game, we came out on the road, we wanted to get at least two out of four, and we ended up getting three out of four, which is great."

O'Brien: "Do you know how many points you scored?"

Jordan: "No, but we won."

O'Brien: "Fifty-nine. Couldn't you get sixty?"

Jordan: "A win, that is all we wanted."

Everything you need to understand Jordan's greatness—beyond his athletic ability—is in this brief interview. First, notice that Jordan used the word "we" six times; he never used the word "I." He cared about the victory in the context of the season. He didn't care about how many points he scored. It was the sports writers who zeroed in on that detail. He was excited about the win. He was excited about his team's success. Jordan was doing everything he could to win, but the victory wasn't his alone, and he knew it.

Jordan—and don't let anyone tell you otherwise—was not a selfish player. He was a ruthless competitor and a superstar of the first magnitude, but he was not selfish. Using your talents fully in service to the team, doing everything you can for your team to win, this is not selfish. In fact, holding talent back is selfish. The most competitive man on the planet is also an unselfish teammate.

Competitiveness, like a lot of mental talents, can be improved and influenced, cultivated. It's determined by your passion, motivation, determination, and discipline.

Ever land on a team with a super-competitive person? Someone who fights for everything? Gives no quarter and goes all out, no matter the odds? It's invigorating. A super-competitive person radiates passion and intensity. You can see their very skull glowing beneath their skin. You can feel their energy coursing through their every move, and that energy is contagious.

Don't underestimate the power of competitiveness. "You can't always be the most talented person in the room," Pat Summit said. "But you can be the most competitive."

TOUGHNESS

Battles with aggression and intensity. Expects all things to be earned and competes with physical tenacity and mental toughness. Thrives under pressure and fights for each other without fear.

Probably the best take on toughness comes from ESPN commentator Jay Bilas, who said that "the tough player is the one who is difficult to play against and easy to play with."

People display toughness all the time, but it appears especially when teams are facing difficulties, obstacles, hurdles, and failure. A lot of people and teams aren't born tough; they have to earn it, develop it and expect it from each other.

And your team can. Toughness—like all the other mental talents in the Extreme Teammate Pyramid—is a learned behavior. And anything that can be learned can be taught.

Toughness is linked to preparation and trust. Physical toughness grows out of hard training and being in the best possible shape. Mental toughness comes out of fighting through exhaustion. It is much, much easier to be tough if you are prepared. Teammates should also be tough on each other. It's one of the best ways to improve individually and as a team, and it's much easier to be tough on someone when they know you care about them.

So, first and foremost: model toughness as a team. Relish the opportunity to compete. Seek out challenges. "I smile at obstacles," Tiger Woods said.

Perseverance is good. Struggle is good. It means the team is engaged in something meaningful. Thomas Paine wrote: "What we obtain too cheap, we esteem too lightly." He was right. The harder the struggle, the sweeter the victory.

Tough teams find a way to fight through the setbacks, unify, and grow stronger. Weak teams tend to wither or fall apart. Embrace these challenges because the most substantial growth always occurs through adversity. In popular culture, this is often referred to as the turning point of a season. So keep in mind that the rough times will only make a tough team stronger.

How does your team react to getting knocked down, to getting punched in the face? Does your team bemoan problems or find solutions? Does your team embrace adversity with optimism? Does your team see struggle as an opportunity?

Collective preparation, collective enthusiasm, collective intelligence, and collective execution result in confidence and toughness.

In my experience, players don't like to hear a coach say "we're going to have a tough practice today." They usually dread it, and who wouldn't? But, I tried something different a few years ago and told the team that we were going to have an "adversity practice." I told them that we were going to challenge their toughness. A simple reframing of the ordeal and, guess what? The players embraced the idea. They saw that we had a purpose.

Being pushed beyond what you think might be your limits is a good thing—the feeling of exhaustion, of wanting to quit, of thinking there's nothing left in the tank but then finding a little bit more. When you push through that desperate feeling of exhaustion to the other side, it builds confidence and toughness and perseverance and character. Pushing each other past the lows, the moments where you are about to throw in the towel and declare defeat, prepares you for the very stuff of life, when the punches are often real.

And going through this process with teammates builds up relationships. You finally realize you can rely on the person to your left, to your right. This is what you have in common—you've been through the valley together and you've made it back to the mountaintop.

EFFORT

Energizes the team with hustle, heart, and courage. Stays in peak condition and does whatever is needed to win. Outworks all opponents and demands a relentless effort from everyone.

Effort boils down to where your team decides to set the thermostat. Do you like to keep it at a cool seventy and be average? Or, do you turn up the heat and set the thermostat to one hundred degrees? Many people are content with the status quo—a balmy seventy. Those same people usually don't realize they have the capacity for a blazing hundred. Remember: nothing really grows in the comfort zone.

Each individual needs to give everything they can, inspiring their teammates to do the same. Yes, effort can fluctuate, but consistency is the goal. We're all human and have private lives. Sometimes it happens that you'll slip down to ninety degrees. This is okay. But that's what extreme teammates are for, to remind you of the mission, to keep you focused, to get you back to a hundred.

Teams that keep the thermostat at a hundred will outwork their opponents, always. Extreme teammates know how to energize each other to ensure that everyone is giving maximum effort. They fight and battle, they encourage with hustle and grit. Their heart and desire shows up through a collaborative effort. If you are the person that always gives 100 percent, congratulations, but realize that just like every other expectation that we have discussed, you are not a master until you demand the same type of effort from other people. It can't be one person doing all the dirty work, it has to be everyone. Each person demands the absolute best from everyone on the team, there is no other way to approach it.

SELFLESSNESS

Sacrifices personal glory for team success. Generates chemistry, strives for unity, and always puts the team before oneself. Plays for each other and is happy when teammates succeed.

Selflessness is the builder of chemistry. It is a state of mind. It's a way of moving through the world. On a team, selflessness means keeping the needs of others in front of your own. It means staying focused on the good of the team. Selflessness is crucial to a successful career.

Being selfish is a cancer. If you are selfish—if you go for the goal when you should have passed the ball—your teammates will be selfish in kind. I've seen teams splinter into factions as individuals pursue stats, personal agendas, and their own glory.

But, if you are selfless, you can influence your entire team to operate as selflessly. It's an amazing dynamic. Basketball great John Wooden said it best: "A player that makes a team great is better than a great player."

There are hundreds of ways to gauge selflessness. For example, think about how a sports team watches film. Watching oneself is important, natural, and necessary. But, do people *only* watch themselves, or do they watch their teammates, too, noticing things and sharing them with each other? Extreme teammates do this because the ultimate goal is team improvement, not just self-improvement. Simply stated, stop trying to prove what *you* can do individually and focus on proving what you can do *together*.

At the team banquet, are people happy when a teammate gets an award? I mean truly happy? If not, re-examine the relationships within the team and the contributions people are making for each other. If people are not happy when a teammate succeeds, there is work to do.

The 1934 St. Louis Cardinals were known as the Gashouse Gang. They won ninety-five games and beat the Detroit Tigers in the World Series. They got their nickname because they were a bunch of rough and tumble, hard-nosed players. Many worked second jobs in the off-season, but they played so well together that they became unbeatable.

Frankie Frisch was a player and the team's manager. Some of the other players included greats such as Dizzy Dean, Leo Durocher, Ripper Collins, Joe Medwick, and Pepper Martin. They were working class joes.

During warm-ups before a playoff game, gloves popping and chatter in the background, a reporter asked Frisch why his team was so good. How do you guys do it? Frisch smiled and then began calling the players over one at a time. He asked each player variations on the same question. "How many hits do you have?" Or, "How many bases did you steal this year?" And each, in turn, including Dizzy and Leo and Ripper and Joe, said the same thing: "I don't know, coach." Over and over. He called his power hitter over and asked him how many home runs he had. "I don't know, coach."

Frisch looked at the reporter, still smiling. "You give me a team of guys like that," he said, "and we'll never lose."

Selfless players don't care about stats or individual accolades. They care about winning, and that's it.

Extreme teammates make extremely successful teams

A team that is loaded with extreme teammates will inevitably become a team that overachieves. These teams have fun together. They build relationships, and they are happy when their teammates succeed because they are invested in each other. They stay hungry, and they fight for one another because they know the value of never giving up. They are accountable to each other, and they enforce standards through shared leadership and collective responsibility. They sacrifice for one another, and they have clear roles that are executed together like a well-oiled machine. They are grateful and forgiving, and they understand that working together is always more powerful than working alone. They have the energy to excel at the end of a season because they have created a culture that suppresses pessimism and feeds optimism. Extreme teammates build their teams through every action, every word, and every decision. Their climate might fluctuate, but each expectation becomes more consistent as skills and talents are developed and the team's culture is maintained.

What it all comes down to is this: how can teammates use their own mental talents to improve the person next to them? How can teams get as many people as possible to master as many mental talents as possible? Use these tools, this framework, these expectations and the sky's the limit, for you and for your team.

Darren Barndt

CHAPTER 8
Do Everything to Win

Sports can be hard on the psyche. They teach us so many things, including how to win with grace, and how to lose with dignity and spirit. But there is a disturbing trend in sports these days, where who wins is secondary to how the players *feel*.

This is crazy. Yes, the primary focus of all youth sports should be to have fun. But the bedrock of sports is winning, whether you are playing little league or major league. By design, sports are set up for one team or person to vanquish another. So— do everything to win. This is the essential goal of this book—to give you a framework, an attitude, a philosophy, and a battle cry— to help you win. Winning is your North Star.

Doing everything to win is the link that binds extreme teammates together. Extreme teammates don't just play to win. They *desperately* want to win. This drives them to do everything in their power, to utilize every resource, within the rules—to win. Wanting and striving to win is what makes us better. The desire for victory is what brings teammates together to overcome obstacles, to overachieve, to pursue greatness.

Losing is a great teacher. There will always be losses. But don't ever let anything distract you from the fact that wanting and striving to win is the ultimate goal.

I believe things like participation trophies, mercy rules, and scoring limits can be harmful. My oldest son is on the high school wrestling team. This is a sport I know very little about, which is probably a good thing for our relationship. But I do know that, among other things, being an excellent wrestler requires an amazing bundle of competitiveness, perseverance, grit, commitment, and mental toughness.

When my son was fifteen, he asked me to drive him to a one-day competition about an hour away. He explained that this off-season event had a reputation for being very competitive. But it's cool, he said. Everyone gets a trophy.

Of all the sports, I thought, why are they giving participation trophies in wrestling? But I remained quiet on our drive.

We arrived. He checked in. I found a spot on the bleachers. The competition began. As the day went on, I watched my son, who is a solid wrestler, get pummeled, over and over again. In match after match, he was absolutely destroyed.

As a coach, I don't know much about wrestling, but I do know a little about grit, intensity, focus, and perseverance. And my son showed absolutely none of it that day. I was disappointed. I was also confused. I knew him to be a tough and dedicated competitor. What was going on?

As the tournament concluded, everyone waited around for their participation trophies while watching the other wrestlers compete in their final rounds. I stood by and contemplated how to handle this one. I envisioned pulling him away before the trophy presentation, not letting him touch something he didn't earn. Or plucking the trophy from his hands and throwing it in the garbage on the way out.

But I knew that whatever I decided to do, he would remember this for a very long time. I didn't want to wound him, but I also didn't want him to learn the wrong lesson and carry that with him forever. So I proceeded with caution.

On the drive home, I asked my son a question I always advocate asking in youth sports: "Did you have fun?"

I was glad to hear him say "no, not really."

I simply nodded, keeping my eyes on the road, and said, "Yeah, you got beat up pretty bad today." I snuck a peak and watched him holding the trophy in his lap. He stared at it with his head down for a long time. I must admit, I briefly thought: here's my chance! I'll throw it out the window to really reinforce my point. But I restrained myself.

A week passed before I asked about the tournament again. I brought it up casually, not mentioning the trophy. This time my son had a different answer: he told me that he realized why he had performed so terribly. He was promised something whether or not he earned it. He had figured this out himself, without any coaxing or prompting or trashing from me. The trophy was still on his shelf, but I was more than proud of him.

Six months later, I wandered into his room to see if that trophy was still on his shelf. I couldn't find it. When I asked him about it, he didn't hesitate: "Oh, I threw that away a while ago."

"Why?" I asked.

"Because I didn't get first, and I didn't earn it."

My son showed the wisdom and understanding that was lacking in the adult who decided to hand out participation trophies at the wrestling tournament. Sports aren't about your feelings. Life isn't about your feelings. Young people need to learn how to cope with losing. If they are sheltered from the pain of defeat, they never learn how to dedicate and commit to something, how to fight for something, how to defy the odds and persevere. If kids aren't allowed to lose, they can't learn from their losses. They can't configure them as a step towards a win. Instead, sheltered from loss, they learn to see their feelings, as opposed to their performance, their effort, their preparation, their competition, as the focus. The thing is, one person's feelings in a giant tournament? They don't amount to much.

I know some people might feel this approach is mean or cold-hearted. It's not. It's honest. Giving trophies to kids at any age for something that they didn't earn doesn't build confidence, it makes confidence superfluous. It doesn't build accountability, responsibility, or character; it creates entitlement. It doesn't establish perseverance, toughness, or courage; it leads to quitting. It doesn't inspire motivation, work ethic, focus, passion, determination, or excellence; it produces complacency.

No one is guaranteed success. You have to go out and earn it.

As Doc Rivers says, "Young players have to be taught to win. They know how to play. They haven't figured out how to do it and win at the same time." Part of your culture is the fire in the belly, the raw desire, the *need* to win. Winning might not be everything, but wanting to win is everything, the whole enchilada. Desire is how we get better, how we make great teams. Desire is human nature. More than anything else, it is what we have in common with each other.

Competing to win is part of everything we do. Going for a new job? You need to triumph over other applicants. Wrote a novel? There are thousands of writers trying to get their books published at the same time. Recorded some music? The internet is deluged with new artists every day. I don't say any of this to discourage anyone. I'm saying that you have to compete in the real world and you learn how to do this best in sports.

Wanting to win creates a timeless framework for pursuing achievement. Wanting to win should be your abiding passion. Doing everything to win forces you to blend physical talent with mental talent. It is the essential piece that holds all twenty-one expectations of mental talents together. Winning isn't the only focus for a team, but it is the glue that binds all the different talents and skills together to fight as a unit.

Winning isn't a bad word. It's a great word.

The talents we use to win in sports when we are young are the talents that will define you throughout your life. Competing in sports gives us the skills to flourish in all of our endeavors that follow.

Every employer wants to know what kind of teammate you'll be. They want to know if you'll value your coworkers. They want to know if you can inspire others. Are you a winner? Are you an overachiever? Are you a competitor? Do you do the extra work? Are you an extreme teammate?

Use the frameworks in this book to become the extreme teammate that everyone wants to hire for their team. Use the frameworks in this book to become a manager who knows how to find and hire the extreme teammates who will make your team great.

I believe that being part of a sports team is one of the best and most profound relationships a person can have. As my own children get older and progress in the sports of their choosing, I see how sports train and mold young people into more resilient and capable young adults. Competition—the drive to win, to be the best—is an essential component.

CHAPTER 9
Measuring Expectations

In any competitive environment, you are always being evaluated. Sometimes the evaluation process is hidden. Sometimes the evaluations are public and brutal. But, whether people realize it or not, formally or informally, fairly or unfairly, they are always being evaluated.

But oftentimes these evaluations are incomplete and inconsistent and fail to actually measure the criteria that are really valued by the team.

In the business world, we typically measure obvious criteria such as productivity, sales, and profits. In sports, most teams evaluate things that are easy to measure such as batting average, steals, points per game, goals, and tackles. Yes, these stats are important. But, as you have learned, the more intangible qualities like perseverance, focus, wellness, passion, character, toughness, selflessness, trust, communication, responsibility, work ethic, enthusiasm, and accountability bring greatness. So, it would be beneficial to measure them.

Measuring these expectations helps build our mental talent. It provides a framework for growth, a roadmap to success, an evaluation checklist to reaching greatness. In order to achieve something, you must define the expectations necessary to get there and then continually measure the progress you've made towards mastering them.

Using the Extreme Teammate Pyramid

The Extreme Teammate Pyramid (in the Appendix) combines the twenty-one essential attributes of success for competitive environments into three areas: foundation, culture, and climate. Every person on the team should have access to these expectations.

Unlike John Wooden's pyramid, this pyramid operates downward. Every expectation is impacted by neighboring expectations vertically. For example, great work ethic builds confidence. Strong trust creates strong commitment. Intelligence comes from application. There are mini pyramids formed within the larger framework. For example, effective application builds intelligence and strong execution.

How to use assessments to measure growth

Great teams don't just happen on their own. They require modeling and measuring. There is a shift in public education that promotes the usage of self-assessments and peer evaluations, even at the elementary level. The theory is that children should be responsible for their own learning, and this is a good theory. So be prepared—these young adults are coming through the system, and they are conditioned to effectively use evaluations and assessments as a mechanism to supplement their own growth; they almost expect it. Embrace this shift now, get ahead of the curve, and your team will gain a competitive advantage.

Because the measurement of your personal and team growth is not just the responsibility of the coaching staff. The team needs to take ownership over this, too. Everyone on the team is in it together, and they should share honest feedback that will make each other better. The best way to know if someone is a great teammate is to ask their teammates.

Once you've begun rewriting and rewiring the culture of your team, you need some way to know if what you are doing is effective. Yes, you can look at the win/loss record from season to season or your team's quarterly sales record, but there are more sophisticated methods of measurement.

Although quantitative improvement—more wins, more sales—is the ultimate goal, it is often not the best way to assess how the team is improving. True competitors will always force themselves to reflect on their performances not only when they lose but also when they win. The final score reflects countless variables that we can't control—luck both good and bad, referees, and so on. We should condition ourselves to reflect through assessment based on whether the team's standards are being achieved on a regular basis. Reflection has to be intentional. The assessments have to be transparent. People have to trust each other to be honest and to listen honestly. You need a method to measure all progress.

And we've got the method—a series of digital assessments created specifically for teams. Use them. They are effective tools. But they are not just measuring for measuring's sake; they are designed to make success happen more quickly.

These frameworks, evaluations, and assessments measure those essential but intangible skills and attributes that are so difficult to measure. They define expectations; they promote honest reflection; they provide transparent assessments and give people the ability to identify their own strengths and weaknesses.

If you measure something successfully, you have a much better chance of managing it effectively. And if you manage something effectively, you have a much better chance of exceeding expectations as an individual and as a team. It's an ongoing process that is developed through intentional practice and structured reflection. You can access our frameworks, evaluations and assessments by simply searching @extremeteammates.

Keep in mind, people stay motivated when they know they are growing. We are always interested in learning more about ourselves. Assessments and evaluations foster that motivation by encouraging people to take ownership of their own growth while actively sharing responsibility for the growth of others. And taking ownership of our personal growth inspires us to take ownership of the team's growth.

CHAPTER 10
Great Teams Impact Humanity

How do you want to be remembered? What do you want your legacy to be? What kind of impact do you want to make?

When you think about these questions, remember that our physical capacity has limits and an expiration date, mental capacity does not. In thirty years, your teammates are going to struggle to remember specific plays or moments in games, even big ones. They'll forget one practice as opposed to another and, in some cases, won't even remember who all was on a specific team.

But your teammates will remember those who helped them. If you stay other-centered, always looking for ways to help your teammates, you will be remembered. If you get to know the passions and dreams of your teammates, you will be remembered. If you influence someone to make better choices, you will be remembered. If you believe in someone, and let them know you believe in them, you will be remembered.

This is the best legacy you can hope for—being remembered for helping others.

Some time ago, I was in downtown Chicago and waiting in a mall for my wife while she shopped. A homeless man approached. There were two comfortable chairs; I was in one, and he sat down in the other one. He asked for money. I said no. So we sat in silence. I knew my wife would be awhile, and I was bored, so I turned to the man next to me, and soon we were talking. We talked about basketball for nearly two hours. And his warmth and knowledge of the game made me feel terrible for being short with him when he first sat down. I misjudged him. I saw the dirty clothes, heard the request for money, and I just wrote him off.

The guy was very intelligent and had great insight into the game. I learned a lot from him. He was so knowledgeable and impressive, if he had been decked out in nice clothes, I would have believed he was a professional scout.

Now here's the thing. This guy had something powerful to give, a mind attuned to a sport I love and coach, but I missed it. I eventually gave him a little cash, but I didn't do anything more. I was selfish and afraid. I was unwilling to try to find a way to impact this guy. And I could've. And should've. I believe the world probably lost a great coach that day.

Martin Luther King Jr. said: "Life's most persistent and urgent question is, 'What are you doing for others?'"

And if it seems like I've strayed from my arguments, I haven't. As important as competition is, being part of a team and being an extreme teammate is about much more than winning. It's about relationships, it's about people, it's about the impact you have on each other, on society, on humanity. Seizing these opportunities to help others just takes an open mind, an acute awareness of possibility, and, most importantly, a commitment to helping others.

Everyone needs a helping hand sometimes. Everyone has challenges. And everyone can find solutions in other people. Be the change, the reason, the difference in a teammate's life. Basketball great Jim Valvano said, "A person really doesn't become whole until he becomes a part of something that's bigger than himself." As a team, your ability to bring people together and propel one another to newer heights by helping each other cultivate your strengths and improve your weaknesses is the very essence of greatness. Working together for each other and for the team—this is what people remember. The impact can last a lifetime.

Improving yourself is good. Improving your community is *necessary*.

A great team can change a town, a city, a nation. Sports matter and great teams resonate. I believe in sports as a way for people to heal, to come together, to overcome.

There are always going to be outside forces working against you. A good example is how we consume information under the guise of the national news media. When the national dialogue is about hate, anger, and division, people tune in to the news. These companies, on both sides, have us at each other's throats to boost their ratings and their profits, and they don't care about the destruction they cause in the process.

Fight back. Tune out the noise, and really see other people. Don't avoid building relationships with teammates who are different from you. Seek them out. Trust is too important to let some profit-driven invisible hand dictate who you will and will not build relationships with. Inquire, share, do the important work that is foundational to relationships between teammates. Remember, you will always have much, much more in common with other people—all the other people on the planet—than you have that's different. The disrupters are out there. Be aware of them; don't let them win.

Great things are happening all over the place that go unrecognized, progress is being made, and often this progress goes unnoticed or intentionally ignored.

The times, to quote Bob Dylan, they are changing. And often for the better.

Yes, there is still much work to do. But *progress is happening*.

And, a good deal of the credit belongs to our love of sports, our love of teams, and our commitment to win something great through collective effort. Sports, more than just about any other area, helped desegregate our country. It was the sports stars—Jackie Robinson, Joe Louis, and so on—who broke through the hard-edged racism of the time and into the hearts of America.

Look at the crowd at any sporting event and you will see people from different backgrounds, different races. And they will all be celebrating, or suffering, together. Sports create a community of fans. And when a team does the hard work to overachieve—when they have created the deep bonds that result in victories—the fans are brought together too. Sports are one of the major ways people track time and think about their own lives. In this country, we do that together more than we do it apart.

So engaging with your teammates and working to become an extreme teammate yourself is not just about the games in front of you. You are—and I am not exaggerating—working to make the world a better place.

Change starts with ideas, with new perspectives. It happens when we find the common good in each other, when we respect each other regardless of skin color, ethnic background, sexual orientation, or gender. Those things don't matter, especially when we are fighting for a common cause—to win, to overachieve together—when we are looking forward instead of backward, when we identify ourselves as people instead of fractured groups, when we truly see the inside of a person instead of the outside of a person.

Horace Mann, the great champion of American public education, admonished: "Be ashamed to die until you have won some victory for humanity." Extreme teammates make great teams. And great teams don't just win victories for themselves, they win for humanity.

Conclusion: The Infinite Power of Teams

Overachievement occurs when every member of the team has the opportunity to utilize their talents. When they leverage those talents and skills to make each other better. When they create a team full of leaders that enforce their own standards. When they use winning as the glue that binds them together.

It took me half a lifetime, but my core beliefs about creating great teams has shifted. Evolved. I finally realized that every single member of a team, from the superstar to the benchwarmer, has the capacity to do two things: contribute to leadership and be a great teammate. With proper expectations, a commitment to excellence, and a willingness to put the team first, every team can and should come to a point where they reach greatness.

Bobby Knight was well known for using every resource at his disposal to drive success in his program. Well, the most overlooked and underutilized resource of any organization is almost always its people. Physical resources, state-of-the-art weight rooms, and twenty-first century facilities definitely help drive success. But in the end, it will always come down to our ability to cultivate and inspire greatness in our teammates. And, the most direct, sure-fire path to make this happen is through our reliance on and commitment to each other, through our collective strengths shared with one common goal in mind: winning.

Physical talent alone is never enough, it never will be. Mastery of physical talent prepares people for games. Mastery of mental talent prepares people for life. Teams that do both have infinite potential. Teams that do both overachieve. Teams that do both move the world forward.

APPENDIX

Team Activities & Inspiration

Shaping a group into a team is a multi-step process, and it takes time. Team-building activities are just one aspect of this process, but they are important.

Soldier Award: A two-cent plastic soldier figurine strung on a necklace or lanyard can go a long way towards developing a team. Designate someone to bestow the award first. This person explains what the award is honoring—it can be given for accomplishments in the weight room, hard work in practice, anything, really. The winner keeps the soldier for a week and then passes it off to a teammate to honor another accomplishment. And so on. This is simple and effective.

Life Story: Speed up the relationship-building process by having everyone share their life story. This works best in a location that is comfortable, safe, and sacred to the team. Make sure you have plenty of time for this activity so no one is rushed. A good facilitator will model sharing their passions, their dreams, their struggles. Everyone must understand and agree that this sharing is confidential and only between members of the team.

One-On-One Challenge: Players choose one person who they don't know very well. They must get to know each other in seven days and be able to share the other person's story with the team. A great prompt is to ask each person to understand the talents, dreams, and passions of the other. This can be refashioned with other prompts and repeated week after week with different pairings, and it's a great way to turn multiple cliques into a whole unit.

Sleepovers: Encourage sleepovers for players who don't know each other well. Don't worry about a schedule; if a player has a band recital in the evening after practice, their teammate should go.

Some players have had sleepovers on a school night just to make sure the other person can experience how life really operates in the world of their teammate.

Two-Minute Sunrise: To better understand the importance of two minutes, whether it's the last two minutes of a game or two minutes in the middle of a practice or in a workout, have your players gather together in a place where they can watch the sunrise and see how quickly things change in two minutes. It's a great team activity that puts the importance of time into great perspective.

Cell Phone Blackout: A great way to build camaraderie through conversation. Ask the team to turn off their phones on the bus rides. This is no joke: The Texas Tech men's basketball team-imposed cell phone blackout times in 2019, and it was the first year they reached the Final Four.

1-3-1: Have you ever spent time to create goals, vision, or mission at the beginning of the season but then failed to revisit it during the season? The 1-3-1 approach is a simple formula that's easy to use, understand, and remember. Come up with one purpose, three goals, and a one-word battle cry.

For example:
1- Purpose: To impact other people
3- Goals: Win regionals, stay in peak shape, improve.
1- One-word battle cry: Fearless!

Hidden Message: Create an acronym that is only shared within the team. For the sample above we would put the letters TIOP on the team's shooting shirts. This stands for "To Impact Other People," a great message that could even go on practice gear. This helps everyone remember what's important and provides a bit of extra camaraderie for the team.

Permissions: This was originally developed by Morgan Wooten, who is considered one of the best high school basketball coaches of all time. Simply give a teammate a "permission" when they do something great in practice. The player can use that permission at the end of practice. So, if the team has ten suicides at the end of a practice, with one permission, a player only needs to do nine suicides. Players could also give their permission to a teammate and run the suicide for them. You could also designate a player to give permissions at each practice.

Snail Mail: Do you want to make sure an important handout resonates with the team? Send it via postal mail. How many people receive something in the mail anymore? Be sure to omit the return address so you can model selfless action for the team.

Quote Share: Have players memorize a favorite quote of a teammate and then recite it to the team before practice starts. This is inspiring but also a great way to know someone better. During pre-season, UNC coach Roy Williams asks his team to memorize some of his favorite quotes, then he randomly chooses one or two players to recite a quote before they are allowed to practice.

Three Best Teammates: Instruct players to write down the three best teammates on the team. Collect all their answers and put all the names on the board. Do this for a couple practices. When players continually do not see their own name on the board, they typically make some changes.

Culture Day: Designate a day where players can have a voice in what to do to improve the team culture. Bring in board games. Have a chess tournament. Visit a children's hospital. Raise money for a homeless person. The men's lacrosse team at the University of Virginia calls it Culture Thursdays.

Bowling Night: Yeah, many teams go bowling, but make it fun and competitive. Designate a couple players to be responsible for coming up with fun awards.

The Foxhole: If you were at war, which teammate would you choose to be in a foxhole with? Have players write their answers down. Write all the names on the board. Repeat in a week to see if new names appear.

Competitive Olympics: The Chicago Bears do something similar but form two teams and create as many competitive games as possible. The games can be goofy but keep them competitive. Example: Rolling a basketball into a trash can, throwing a football to knock over cones, a golf-putting contest, baseball bat relays, tug of war. Players love this stuff, especially during the grind of a season, and cross-training is a great way to beef up a team.

The Power Card: Buzz Williams uses this approach with his team. Simply print some business cards with your team logo and add different quotes or power statements, and laminate them. Give one to a player to make a point and drive motivation. For example, a card could say: "You have been doing great things lately, I believe in you." It's a small gesture with a big impact.

Partner Bonding Questions: Great for culture day. Have players partner up and take five to ten minutes for people to share the answer to some relationship-building questions. Here are a few examples:

- If you could have a personal billboard display a message with twenty-five words or less, what would it say?
- What is your biggest passion in life that some people may not know?
- If you could play in a golf foursome with anyone dead or alive, what other three people would you choose?
- Which sports franchise would you own, and what would be your focus for the organization?
- What is one place you want to travel to, and why?
- Who is the one person you admire most, and why?
- What is one of the most challenging things you have ever done?
- If you could live in any country for the rest of your life where would it be, and why?
- Who was one of your favorite coaches or teachers, why?
- If you were in a band, what would be your role?

- What are three things you want to accomplish in life?
- If you wrote a book, what would be the title? What would it be about?
- What is something that you think everyone should do at least once? Why?
- What is something that you have tried and would never do again? Why?
- If you had a time machine, would you go back in time or into the future? Why?

There are many, many others. Don't avoid these because they are honest and open. Don't think that your teammates will be cynical. Everyone has a story to share and wants a chance to tell it. Everyone wants to be accepted. Extreme teammates build up their team culture all the time.

Team Inspiration:

Sharing a simple poem, quote, or short story is a great strategy for middle-of-the-week practices or meetings. This can occur before or after practice or in a one-minute break during practice. In my experience, the most effective scenario is when the team takes a short break during a tough part of practice and a member of the team reads a short story or poem aloud.

<u>A Tale of Two Wolves</u>

An old Cherokee sat his grandson down one day and decides to pass along some wisdom about life. He pointed to his chest. "A fight is going on inside me," he said to the boy.

"It is a terrible fight and it is between two wolves. One is evil—he is anger, envy, sorrow, regret, greed, arrogance, self-pity, guilt, resentment, inferiority, lies, false pride, superiority, and ego." He continued, "The other is good – he is joy, peace, love, hope, serenity, humility, kindness, benevolence, empathy, generosity, truth, compassion, and faith. The same fight is going on inside you – and inside every other person, too."

The grandson thought about it for a minute and then asked his grandfather, "Which wolf will win?"

The old Cherokee simply replied, "The one you feed."

If You Think You Can
If you think you are beaten, you are;
If you think you dare not, you don't!
If you'd like to win, but you think you can't,
It's almost certain you won't.
If you think you'll lose, you're lost;
For out in the world we find
Success begins with a fellow's will;
It's all in the state of mind!
If you think you're outclassed, you are;
You've got to think high to rise.
You've got to be sure of yourself
Before you 'll ever win the prize.
Life's battles don't always go
To the stronger or faster man;
But sooner or later the man who wins
Is the person who thinks he can!
—*Author Unknown*

Life is a Gift
Life is a gift, to be used every day,
Not to be smothered, and hidden away.
It isn't a thing, to be put in a chest,
Where you put all your keepsakes, and treasure your best.
It isn't a thing to be used now and then,
And promptly put back in the dark again.
Life is a gift, even the humblest may boast of,
So, keep it and use each hour of the day,
And you'll find that in use, it gets better in every way.
—*Author Unknown*

Effort and Success

In the battle of life, it is not the critics who count: not the man who points out how the strong man stumbled, or where the doer of a deed could have done better. The credit belongs to the man who is actually in the arena: whose face is marred by dust and sweat and blood; who strives valiantly; who errs and comes short again and again because there is no effort without error and shortcoming; who does actually strive to do the deeds: who knows the great enthusiasms, the great devotion, spends himself in a worthy cause; who at best knows in the end the triumph of high achievement; and who at worst if he fails, at least fails daring greatly, so that his place shall never be with those cold and timid souls who know neither victory nor defeat.

- *Theodore Roosevelt*

Don't Quit

When things go wrong as they sometimes will
When the road you're trudging seems all uphill
When the funds are low and the debts are high
And you want to smile, but you have to sigh
When care is pressing you down a bit
Rest, if you must, but don't you quit
Success is failure turned inside out
The silver tint of the clouds of doubt
And you never can tell how close you are
It may be near when it seems afar
So stick to the fight when you're hardest hit
It's when things seem worst that you mustn't quit
—*Author Unknown*

<u>Winners vs. Losers</u>

A winner works harder than a loser and has more time;
A loser is always "too busy" to do what is necessary.

A winner gets through problems;
A loser goes around it, and never gets past it.

A winner makes commitments;
A loser makes promises.

A winner takes responsibility for mistakes even when they are not his own;
A loser will always find someone else to blame.

A winner says, "I'm good, but not as good as I ought to be;"
A loser says, "I'm not as bad as a lot of other people."

A winner listens;
A loser just waits until it's his turn to talk.

A winner respects those who are superior to him and tries to learn
something from them;
A loser resents those who are superior to him and tries to find clinks in their
armor.

A winner feels responsible for more than his job;
A loser says, "I only work here."

A winner says, "There ought to be a better way to do it;"
A loser says, "That's the way it's always been done here."

A winner finds opportunity in all situations;
A loser never appreciates the chances and freedoms of life.

> - *Pat Williams, NBA General Manager & Vice President*
> *Modified by Darren Barndt with permission from Pat Williams*

10 Ways to Respect Officials & Umpires
By Darren Barndt

1- Play Hard: People officiate and umpire because they love the game. They appreciate teams that give great effort because it epitomizes what sports are about.

2- Build Respect & Rapport: Help with the management of the game. Get foul balls, hustle after loose balls, hand the ball to officials or umpires.

3- Play Through Bad Calls: Focus on what you can control, not what you can't control. Good teams never let a bad call be the reason to lose focus.

4- Respect the Game: Officials reward good team play when it's earned. Play the game knowing the game is always bigger than you or your team.

5- Protect Teammates: Redirect, move or control teammates after bad calls. Only designated players should communicate with officials.

6- Always Hustle: Hustle everywhere, between innings, during timeouts, even when it's not expected. This demonstrates respect for the game.

7- Show Positive Body Language: You're communicating everything through body language. Hand gestures or slouching are signs of selfishness.

8- Be Accountable: Teams have more success when they are accountable. Blaming an umpire or official destroys accountability.

9- Build Your Reputation: You are creating a reputation by how you handle adversity. Do you complain or play for the love of the game?

10- Let the Coach Work: Coaches have a plan for interacting with umpires or officials. If parents, fans or players complain, you are disrupting that process.

EXTREME TEAMMATES
By Darren Barndt

CLIMATE

CULTURE

FOUNDATION

FOUNDATION

CULTURE

CLIMATE

WELLNESS
Makes wise choices. Achieves balance and joy from exercise, nutrition, education, rest and quality time with teammates, family and friends. Is thankful and forgiving. Impacts people with generosity and service.

CHARACTER
Acts with self-control, civility, humility and professionalism. Influences others with honor and integrity and stands up for what is right. Contributes to humanity with kindness, compassion and courage.

TRUST
Has faith in the program and believes in the process. Uses honesty and love to create a system of loyalty, trust and pride. Builds relationships, forms friendships and instills bonds between all people.

COMMITMENT
Is devoted to a shared vision and a greater purpose. Sets high expectations and fully commits to one's role, to the process and to the team. Is dedicated to reaching goals and helping others achieve.

PASSION
Pursues legacy with positive energy, optimism and a fierce desire to be great at what is loved. Builds team pride and cares about team success. Supports the dreams and passions of teammates.

RESPONSIBILITY
Is prompt and reliable. Does not blame others or tolerate excuses. Promotes collective responsibility and shares leadership duties with the team. Influences teammates by modeling responsibility.

ACCOUNTABILITY
Takes ownership of the team by enforcing team standards. Holds people accountable, leads by example, reinforces team expectations and excels in assigned role. Demands accountability from others.

WORK ETHIC
Improves skills with efficient, intelligent and uncomfortable hard work. Gets better every day and creates good habits from repetition, attention to detail and discipline. Pushes others and builds work ethic.

MOTIVATION
Is self-driven, ambitious and an inspiration for hope. Uses unfairness, oversights and failure as motivation. Chases excellence with determination and patience. Over-prepares so the team overachieves.

COMMUNICATION
Speaks with truth and dignity. Uses positive words, shows good body language, listens to understand and doesn't let people complain or criticize. Demands transparency and respect in communication.

FOCUS
Visualizes perfection and success. Uses a clear mind-set to concentrate, relax and focus on achieving specific tasks. Avoids distractions and keeps everyone focused on roles, goals and mission.

PERSEVERANCE
Never gives up. Embraces and faces adversity and uses setbacks as opportunities to get stronger. Competes with a forward thinking attitude and challenges teammates to overcome difficulties.

CONFIDENCE
Has unshakable confidence from total preparation. Makes teammates better and plays with poise and composure. Strongly believes in oneself and makes other people believe in themselves.

ENTHUSIASM
Uses a positive attitude to solve problems, encourage teammates and keep things fun. Brings out the best in people, spreads positivity and inspires the team with a contagious spirit.

APPLICATION
Is coachable, curious and reflective. Listens, observes, applies instruction and uses feedback. Takes risks and learns from mistakes. Asks questions and accelerates growth by teaching others.

ROLE EXECUTION
Achieves synergy when all roles are executed together with perfection. Pushes the group to execute each role with continuity and perform with consistency. Becomes an unstoppable machine.

COMPETITIVENESS
Finds a way to win. Uses inner strength, will power and a competitive drive to rise to the occasion and conquer team expectations. Gets people to compete at their highest level

TOUGHNESS
Battles with aggression and intensity. Expects all things to be earned and competes with physical tenacity and mental toughness. Thrives under pressure and fights for each other without fear

EFFORT
Energizes the team with hustle, heart and courage. Stays in peak condition and does whatever is needed to win. Outworks all opponents and demands a relentless effort from everyone.

SELFLESSNESS
Sacrifices personal glory for team success. Generates chemistry, strives for unity and always puts the team before oneself. Plays for each other and is happy when teammates succeed.

114

Made in the USA
Monee, IL
18 January 2020